The Hungry Spork

The Hungry Spork

A Long Distance Hiker's Guide to Meal Planning

Inga Aksamit

The Hungry Spork

Contact: www.ingasadventures.com

Published by Pacific Adventures Press

Photos by Inga Aksamit, unless otherwise credited

Cover photo: Bullfrog Lake by Inga Aksamit

Cover design by Monique Meade, tastydesign.biz

Dedication

Dedicated to Steve Mullen,
my partner in love, life and adventure. After all, he has to eat the food.

Acknowledgements

I'd like to thank Molly Kurland and Norma Smith Davis for patiently reading all my iterations, and to Crissi Langwell and Laura Hovden for providing expert editing. Monique Meade's creative input on the cover design was invaluable. Aaron Owens, a Registered Dietician and long-distance hiker (she's hiking the PCT in 2017!), kindly reviewed the nutrition chapter. I owe a huge debt of gratitude to these recipe testers from the "Ladies of the JMT" Facebook Group, many of whom went out on a limb to carry food on trips in the hopes that it would taste good on the trail: Kathy Hoffman, Sally Andring Barnhart, Charissa Doerbecker, Juli Wolter, Stacey Less, Celeste Lee Wong, Tami Langer Collard, Deanna Austin, Doreen & Liz Likness, Haley Sankey, and Holly Maszk. A big thank you goes to Sarah Kettles, Valerie Gould Eaton and Jessica Scott for sharing photos and to Tracy Johnson for sharing an important dessert recipe and photos. I would be remiss if I didn't acknowledge all of my imaginary friends in the many hiking groups I belong to on Facebook and other digital sites. I have learned so much from so many and I pass along these tips to others to share the knowledge.

Disclaimer

Hiking and backpacking can be risky endeavors. Preparing, packaging and storing food for a thru-hike involves a certain amount of risk since refrigeration is not available and sanitation may be compromised. Use your best judgment and proper discretion when preparing or consuming any food. You understand and agree that your use of The Hungry Spork is entirely at your own risk.

I am not a certified nutritionist or registered dietitian and make no claims to the contrary. Each individual's dietary needs and restrictions are unique to the individual. Information is provided to the best of my ability. This shouldn't be a surprise, but statements within this site have not been evaluated or approved by the Food and Drug Administration. Content should not be considered a substitute for professional advice. YOU are ultimately responsible for all decisions pertaining to your health.

The nutritional information for recipes is provided as a courtesy and should not be construed as a guarantee. This information is a product of several online calculators. I attempted to provide accurate nutritional information, but these figures should be considered estimates. Varying factors such as product types or brands purchased, natural fluctuations in produce, and the way ingredients are processed change the effective nutritional information in any given recipe. Furthermore, different online calculators provide different results depending on their own nutrition fact sources and algorithms. Under no circumstances will I be responsible for any loss or damage resulting for your reliance on this nutritional information.

Table of Contents

Introduction

This book grew from a personal account of my strategy for planning meals for the John Muir Trail, a 211-mile trek in California. I found meal planning to be overwhelming. I consistently underestimated the time it would take to plan, prepare and package the food required to nourish my husband and me for more than three weeks on the trail. Of course, some superhuman people can shop on Monday, package everything on Monday night and mail out their resupply containers Tuesday morning. More often, though, those people are the ones posting Facebook photos at 3 a.m. surrounded by cardboard boxes and zip-top baggies, their kitchen covered in a fine film of powdered milk, their bodies a heap of sobbing protoplasm. Do yourself a favor and provide good chunks of time to plan your meals.

After hiking all day I'm tired. My goals are to erect my shelter, get cleaned up at a nearby river or lake, eat and sleep. As much as I enjoy cooking in real life, I have little enthusiasm for complicated meal prep after a long day on the trail. I found many books with backcountry recipes that weren't congruent with the way I eat or were too much work to prepare in the field. I was flummoxed by instructions for preparing ovens for bread, packing separate meal ingredients, and cooking on a skillet. We tried cooking (simmering or frying) at the start of our backpacking days and quickly abandoned that due to the mess and trouble. It wasn't our style. We transitioned to "freezer-bag cooking" where food isn't really cooked; it's rehydrated in a plastic bag or pot. On the trail, all I want to do is pour water over my food and eat dinner a few minutes later. Just because the process of rehydrating food is simple, however, doesn't mean it's easy or fast to put together beforehand. Commercial freeze-dried meals are available and were fine when we started backpacking. After a while, though, I wanted food that was more nutritious, had fewer additives and tasted as good as what we make at home.

"It takes time to plan and prepare healthy, flavorful food, but the result is worth it."

If you've read my book, *Highs and Lows on the John Muir Trail*, you know I suffered through the first day of my hike with a migraine. I've always preferred a healthy diet, but trying to modify my diet to reduce migraines took me to a whole new level. I had trouble finding trail foods that didn't contain MSG, nitrates, nitrites, tyramine and other substances that I was trying to limit. It was hard for me because I'm usually an "eat everything" kind of person. I developed a greater appreciation for diabetics, gluten-sensitive individuals and those who choose restricted diets for lifestyle choices. Another issue I have to deal with is altitude. I often backpack at high altitude in the Sierra Nevada and other mountains, and sometimes have low-grade nausea or a suppressed appetite until I acclimate. It has taken a lot of trial and error to learn what foods my stomach will accept.

I try to balance the competing goals, each of which is equally important: fast, wholesome and high-energy while still being tasty.

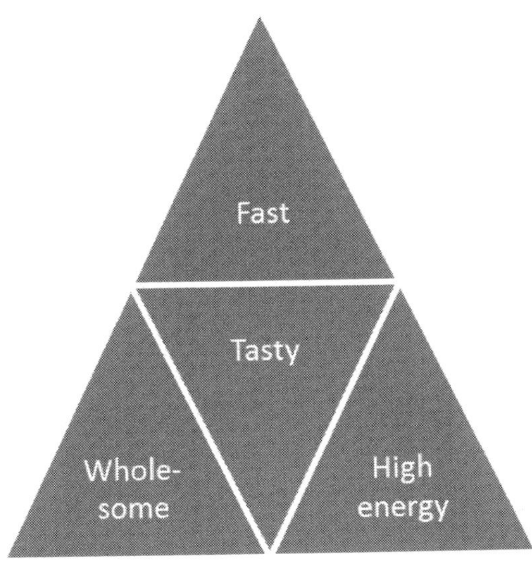

Many popular diets that restrict one food or food group stray far from basic principles of nutrition. There's nothing wrong with any food philosophy as long as you get the nutrients you need. I've relaxed my restricted diet since it didn't improve my migraines, but I'm still a healthy eater. We all have biases and different points of view. Here are a few of my preferences that shape my food choices at home and on the trail.

- I'm an omnivore but favor chicken and fish, eating little red meat.
- I love lots of fruits and vegetables.
- Grains are a staple in my diet, including white, brown and wild rice, quinoa, couscous and other grains.
- Beans are a favorite, usually prepared from dried beans.
- Mashed potatoes are always welcome.
- I like flavorful food from around the world.
- I try to choose minimally processed foods without many additives and preservatives though some processing is often required to make food trail-stable.
- My meals draw from all the food groups and I make sure I get enough protein, carbohydrates and fats.

I tried dehydrating whole meals but found it time-consuming. I worried that if dehydrated mixed meals contained fat or oil, they might go rancid. My meal planning evolved to preparing meals from freeze-dried foods or ingredients I dehydrated at home separately. That way I could control the quality and set up an assembly line. I could prepare many meals in one day as opposed to cooking a single recipe and dehydrating it. It turned out to be more efficient and less time consuming.

Cooking in a pot expands your choices, but it requires more clean-up and isn't as appealing to me as freezer-bag cooking. All the recipes presented here can be heated in a pot, if you prefer. If you are looking for recipes for meals that are cooked at camp (e.g. meals that need simmering), see my resource list in the back for other cookbook suggestions.

There are lots of ways to pull meals together for a multi-week hike, whether it's the John Muir Trail (JMT), Pacific Crest Trail (PCT), Appalachian Trail (AT), Continental Divide Trail (CDT) or other long trek. The extreme ultralight backpackers often don't bring a stove. They forego hot drinks and warm meals, often subsisting on energy bars. Others bring regular food and cook as they do at home. When we were on the Chilkoot Trail in Alaska, two young men pulled out a box of pasta, unwrapped a glass jar of marinara sauce and boiled up a yummy meal of spaghetti. It looked delicious but was hardly practical due to the weight and fragility of the glass jar, not to mention the amount of fuel it takes to boil pasta. Two friends of ours cook up a big batch of stew before embarking on a backpacking trip. They dehydrate it and happily eat the exact same thing every single day. Not me.

This book is not a comprehensive treatise on all aspects of food preparation for backpacking, but provides a system for planning. It's not a guide to dehydrating your own food, though dehydration is one means to create healthy meals. Though my suggestions can't replace advice from a physician or dietician, I offer a strategy for making your own meals so you control the ingredients. It's more than a cookbook, though I do include a chapter with my favorite recipes.

In many cases, generic foods and products recommended or mentioned in this book are produced by multiple manufacturers, brands and retailers. Your choice may be dictated by local or regional availability, though almost everything can be purchased online these days. I mention our favorite products because I get a lot of requests for this information. I have not tested every brand out there and there may be perfectly acceptable alternatives. Check the Appendix for lists of some of the products mentioned in the book. For the most part, I do not receive any payment for recommending products, though I am an Amazon Associates member and sometimes even reach the threshold to get a small payment.

In this book I'll show you my approach to planning meals with trail-tested ideas for food choices. It's a flexible system so you will be able to adapt it to your needs and preferences. My focus is on healthy, nourishing foods that can sustain a long hike, provide variety and be prepared quickly at camp.

Chapter 1: Three Food Strategies

You have your permit in hand and you've gathered your backpacking gear. Now what? The daunting task looms large: how to organize your food for the weeks or months you will be on the trail. Whether you're hiking the 211-mile John Muir Trail (JMT) or one of the longer trails, there is much planning to do. On the Appalachian Trail (AT), hikers only have to carry 3-6 days of food because there are many towns and resupply stops along the way. On the Pacific Crest Trail (PCT) it's 4-10 days between resupply. There are several resupply locations along the JMT (which forms one section of the PCT), but in the southern half the terrain becomes more rugged and resupply options are limited. On one of the longest sections, between Mount Whitney and Muir Trail Ranch, most hikers going at a moderate pace find they must carry approximately a ten day supply of food.

Making sure you have adequate calories, nutrition and variety can be intimidating. Some people are lucky. They can eat the same food day after day, not lose their appetite and never tire of it. They regard food as fuel and that's it. Unfortunately, I'm not one of those people. When I exert myself in vigorous exercise for hours on end, I lose my appetite. As soon as I hit 10,000 feet of elevation, my appetite vanishes because of mild altitude sickness. If I eat the same thing day after day, I start to gag at the thought of it. For a weekend jaunt that's OK. I can survive on my fat stores for a while. I learned that winging it didn't work for me on an eight-day trek across California on the High Sierra Trail. By day six I was starving and nothing in my food barrel was appetizing. I craved protein and salty foods, not the sweet things I had brought and certainly not the brand of energy bars I had with me.

When I was planning for over three weeks on the JMT I knew I'd have to pay close attention to food. I needed to balance nutrients and have more variety so I'd be able to eat. I also had to change my attitude. Food is fuel. If I don't get enough calories, I lack the energy to climb the big mountains. Therefore, I have to eat whether I want to or not. I have to force myself to eat all of the foods I planned for each day before I go to bed. Period. The strategy I've honed over 15 years of backpacking might not work for everyone, but it can benefit many. The result that showed that my strategy worked on the JMT was that I only lost 3 pounds after hiking for 23 days and was never hungry. Even though my husband, Steve, isn't as finicky as I am, he appreciated the tasty food, and it added to our enjoyment of the trail.

Do other backpackers face challenges planning their food for a long hike? We can gain insight by looking at a few data points from John Ladd's annual survey, "Prevalence and severity of 42 challenges and problems among 1,286 John Muir Trail hikers in 2015" (bit.ly/JMTproblems2015) In this survey, three food–related issues were raised. These were each rated a "significant problem" (rating it as 3-5 on a 5 point scale, with 5 being the most significant) by a portion of respondents:

- Hard to eat all the food I carried – 21%
- Food I wanted to carry would not fit in bear canister – 20% (applies to hikers on the entire JMT)
- Hunger or not enough food – 10%

In 2016, the results among 1001 respondents were similar, except the question about fitting food in the canister was asked only of a subset of 100 hikers:

- Hard to eat all the food I carried – 25%
- Food I wanted to carry would not fit in bear canister – approximately 40% (only applied to hikers in the southern half of the JMT where long distances separate convenient resupply locations)
- Hunger or not enough food – 17%

We don't know the reasons for not being able to eat all the food carried, but we can speculate that appetite might be suppressed, food choices might not be palatable or that the person over-planned for the amount of food they might need. Not being able to fit food into the bear canister supports the need to repackage food, but could also be due to requiring more food for the days planned. Hunger or not enough food might reflect a lack of planning or could be due to the restricted space in the bear canister. Regardless of the reasons, the survey results point to the importance of food planning.

The Three Strategies

There are three basic strategies to plan food for a long journey.

- Buy commercial freeze-dried meals, perhaps supplemented with additional ingredients
- Dehydrate whole meals you cook at home, then dry in the oven or dehydrator
- Buy freeze-dried foods or dry your own component ingredients to assemble your own recipes

All three strategies are discussed in more detail below. Sources for obtaining food and equipment can be found in the Appendix.

Steve prepares a freeze-dried lunch on top of Mt. Whitney

Strategy 1. Buy Commercial Freeze-Dried Meals

This is the best strategy for those who are short on time and long on funds. It's also good for people who don't like to cook and/or don't have the patience to fuss with meal prep and dehydrating their own foods. There is still some work involved as many people need to repackage their food so it will fit in the bear canisters that are required in many areas. Repackaging is addressed in Chapter 2. As long as you're repackaging, you might as well add additional ingredients to improve flavor, texture and nutrition.

I have found that supplementing commercially prepared meals is a good way to improve taste, add variety and boost protein levels. Many commercial dinners are skimpy in protein and calories. Adding specific ingredients is a way to balance the nutrients. Most people who decide to purchase commercial meals do so for dinners, though some also obtain packaged breakfasts and lunches.

Buying freeze-dried food is the fastest method. Shop online and place an order in a few minutes or visit a large outdoor retailer to purchase what you need. You'll probably also need to shop at a grocery store for some foods, including drinks and lunch items, but this could be done in less than one day. Repackaging could take another day. As a rough estimate, this method could take around two days total for a month-long trip, longer for a multi-month trip. Many food sources are listed in the Appendix.

Here are a few ideas of foods to add to commercial meals:

Freeze-Dried Veggies

Add individual or mixed vegetables to commercial dinners, which sometimes can be too soupy. It's more efficient to use mixed veggies, but individual veggies can create more variety on the trail. Corn is good with Mexican foods, peas go well with gravies, tomato slices are a natural fit for Italian foods and mixed veggies are good in stews.

Freeze-Dried Fruit

Fruit, which adds sweetness and sometimes a zing of tartness, may be added to cereal, oatmeal or savory grains. They can also be eaten as a snack. Dried fruit, such as apricots, dates and raisins can be used, but they are much heavier than freeze-dried fruit.

Freeze-Dried Meats

Freeze-dried meat (available in bulk cans) is a good addition to increase calories and protein to a ready-made meal. Sausage crumbles are tasty in Italian dinners while ground beef, chicken or turkey can be added to dinners that already contain those items.

Protein Powders

Protein powders, available at grocery stores and natural food stores, may be added to trail shakes, instant breakfast mixes and electrolyte powdered drinks.

Spices and Condiments

Salt and pepper are the minimum components to a spice kit. Those who appreciate some heat will benefit from carrying a small container of red pepper flakes. Ray Rippel, author of *Planning Your Thru-Hike of the John Muir Trail* (jmtbook.com), says, "I am a big believer in carrying fresh jalapeños. Obviously, the heat isn't for everyone, but I find that a little chopped jalapeño put into a dish – even one that does not usually lend itself to a pepper – makes the entire meal taste fresher." Beyond that, spices can be added when repackaging, but make sure you're not overdoing it. Bland meals can be improved with a spice mix such as an Italian blend, Mexican blend, Indian masala or curry, African harissa or others. Herb and spice mixes can be packaged in 3" x 2" zip-top pill pouches, available at pharmacies and online (look for the thicker 3- or 4-mil plastic pouches). Some people bring soy sauce, Sriracha sauce, mustard or other condiment packets, which can be purchased individually. See the Appendix for sources.

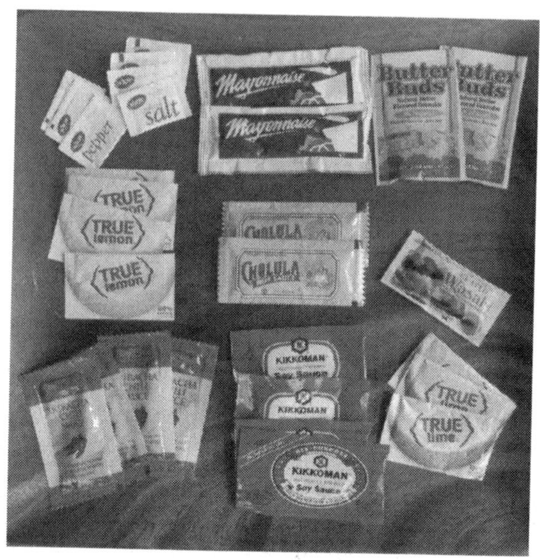

Flavorings and condiments can spice up a meal

Nuts and seeds

Add nuts and seeds to cereals and tortilla fillings to add flavor, nutrition and crunch. Many backpacking foods are soft, so adding texture can increase the palatability, not to mention the nutritional value, of the trail diet.

There are several popular brands of commercial freeze-dried foods, each with their supporters and detractors. Mountain House has become our standby due to its wide availability and variety of meals. I've also enjoyed Backpacker Pantry meals and find them comparable to Mountain House. Backpacker Pantry also has some foods that meet the requirements of certain restrictive diets. Alpine Aire is a brand that has improved a lot over the last few years. A popular choice is Packit Gourmet and their freeze-dried food is undeniably more flavorful and complex, but it is also more expensive than the others. Mary Jane's Organics dinners are a good choice for vegetarians. See the Appendix for more choices.

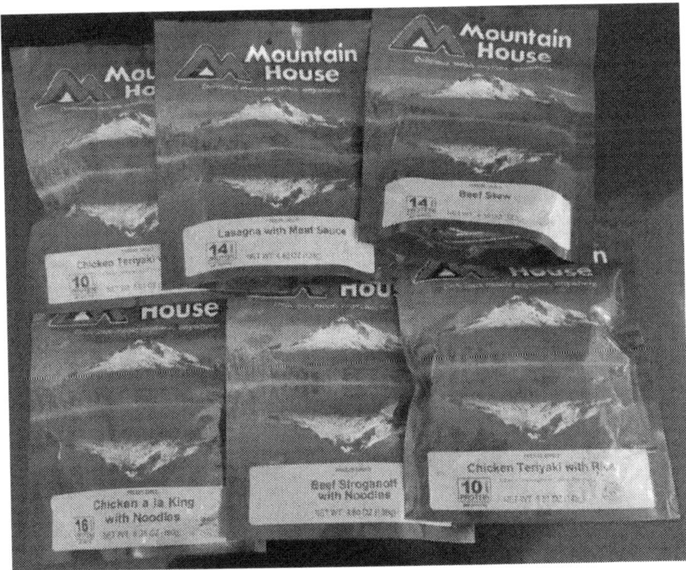

Mountain House freeze-dried meals come in an assortment of flavors

Strategy 2. Dehydrate Whole Meals

Dehydrating your own food has many benefits. It can reduce the cost of your backpacking diet, but it is time consuming. It is not the safest option for very long hikes due to the presence of oils and fats in most meals. Home dehydrated meat should not be stored at room temperature longer than two to eight weeks, depending on how it was prepared.

If you like to cook, have the time and are very organized you can dehydrate some or all of your food for trips of a few weeks. Dehydrating your own food opens a couple of avenues for menu planning. You can prepare whole meals, just as you do now, and dehydrate the meal. A popular method is to make a double batch of a meal, serve one half for dinner and dehydrate the other. Many one-pot meals are suitable for this method. I've listed some recipe ideas for one-pot meals in Chapter 12. However, if you don't usually cook one-pot meals, this method might not be efficient. Another option is to dehydrate individual foods, such as meat or vegetables, to create meals from dry ingredients. See Strategy 3 for more on that.

If you dehydrate much of your own food in whole meals for a three week trip, you could prepare 21 meals at home and have quite a variety. Doubling or tripling a recipe can result in several meals. Most people dehydrate dinners only and use other strategies for breakfast and lunch. The time involved could vary significantly. Efficiency is built in if the same meal is being consumed the night it's prepared, besides being used for the trail. It could range from 10-30 hours or more (much more if you're preparing large batches of food just for the trip) for a four-week trip. This includes shopping, prep time, setting up the dehydrator and packaging. The dehydrator may run for many hours over several weeks, but that doesn't take much time to monitor.

I dehydrated a few meals for backpacking but was put off by one meal that tasted like it was getting rancid. I still dehydrate some individual foods but have found that freeze-dried foods are usually a better fit for my style of food preparation.

Dehydrator

The first step is to acquire a food dehydrator. If you don't have a dehydrator, you can experiment using a convection oven or any oven at the lowest temperature setting. This will take longer and you'll want the efficiency of a dehydrator if you will be drying large volumes of food. Dehydrators blow warm air from a fan through stacks of trays to remove moisture from food. The trays have open spaces to allow air to flow, and inserts can be used for crumbly food (finer mesh) or puree (solid plastic).

There are several brands, but the most popular brands in the U.S. are Excalibur—the Cadillac of dehydrators, and Nesco—the dehydrator for the budget-conscious. Both are excellent quality and the choice depends on your level of funding and what features you want, including timers and temperature control. I have a Nesco Pro without a timer and it works fine for my needs. It's well under $100, while Excalibur can run well above $200.

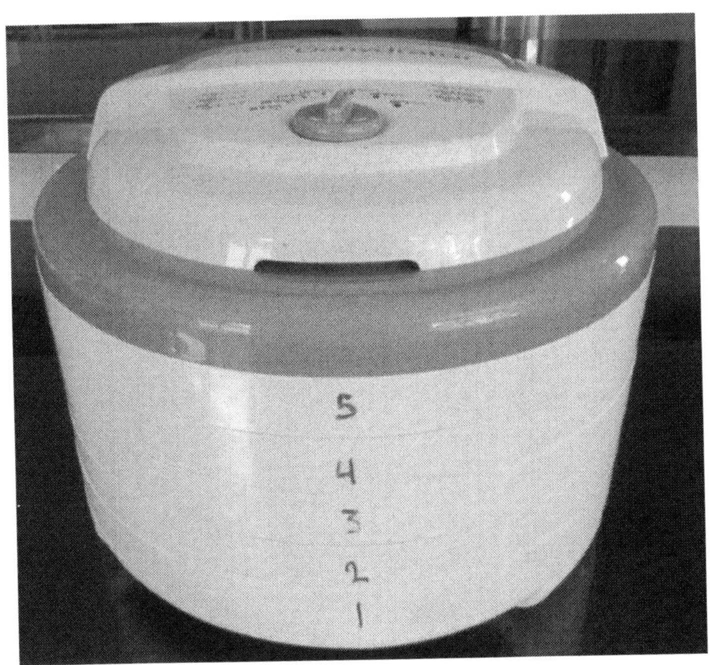

Nesco Pro dehydrator with five round trays

Detailed instructions about how to dehydrate foods are beyond the scope of this book. Excellent instructions can be found at Backpacking Chef(www.backpackingchef.com), along with other resources listed in Appendix 1.

Here are some general tips to get you started.

Safe dehydration practices

Food must be dehydrated properly to prevent illness. The last thing you want to see when you open your resupply box is a large bloom of fluffy green mold. Vegetables that have been properly dried will be brittle while fruit will feel like leather. When drying meat, cook it first and make sure the temperature is maintained at 145 degrees F for 4-6 hours when dehydrating. Ground meat will be hard, similar to gravel. Food safety experts caution that home dehydrated meat is only stable for two weeks without refrigeration, so this is not the best choice for hikes that last months. Freeze-dried meat is a better option for long hikes.

Prevent rancid meat

Use lean meats, trim visible fat and drain fat after cooking. Fat is the cause of rancid meat. I cook ground meat in the skillet, drain the fat and rinse it under running water in a colander to remove as much fat as possible. Dehydrating canned food, bottled sauces or mixed meals such as stews or stir fry is sometimes compromised by fat. It is OK for short-term use, but quality may suffer after long-term storage.

Package and store dehydrated foods

Properly dried food will last for months if vacuumed-sealed and frozen after dehydrating. After removing food from the dehydrator, allow it to cool for 30 minutes, then package. If you leave the food at room temperature in the open for a long time, it will reabsorb moisture.

If you're dehydrating food for use within a couple of weeks, you can store food in a zip-top bag. You can also add oxygen-absorber packets, if desired. If you'll be storing food longer than a year, vacuum-sealing and freezing until needed is recommended. Home vacuum-sealer machines are available that extract the air out of special plastic bags (see Supply List in Appendix 4).

Properly dehydrated jerky can be stored for up to a year if refrigerated or frozen, but should be used within two-eight weeks when unrefrigerated, depending on how it is prepared.

Freezing halts the biological processes that lead to spoilage. I play it safe and freeze my dehydrated food until I need to pack it or mail it for resupply.

See Appendix 1 for more information about food safety with home-dehydrated foods.

Strategy 3. "Buy or Dry" Ingredients to Assemble Meals

An intermediate strategy is to "buy or dry" separate ingredients to create meals from scratch. You can either purchase freeze-dried ingredients in bulk, use your dehydrated ingredients or do a combination of both. They are likely to be more tasty, nutritious and calorie-dense than commercial foods.

Many thru-hikers find that dehydrating components separately allows more flexibility in creating meals compared to dehydrating an entire mixed meal. It's an efficient way to approach meal planning. Large quantities of a specific food can be dehydrated at once without a lot of preparation, measuring, mixing and recipe-following. Over the winter months I'll sauté a big batch of ground beef, turkey or lamb, dehydrate, vacuum seal and pop it in the freezer. I'll do the same with grains, fruits and vegetables. When the weather warms up and I'm ready to plan a backpacking trip, I'll assemble meals from my dehydrated stash, combining them with freeze-dried ingredients, spices and condiments. See comments under Strategy 2 regarding safety.

If you buy freeze-dried ingredients, you can shop online and place an order for bulk cans in a few minutes. You may find bulk cans at a large outdoor retailer, but most only carry small packages of meals. You'll probably want to shop at a grocery store for some foods, including, rice, beans, grains, drinks and lunch items. If you dehydrate your own components, it could take almost as long as strategy #2, but with the benefit of not having to cook a whole recipe. For example, all you have to do is simply open a package of ground beef, cook and dehydrate.

Unlike buying ready-made meals, it does take time to assemble recipes. Dinners could be assembled in a long day while breakfasts and lunches can be prepared in less than a day each for a month-long trip. I found that doing breakfasts one day (or weekend) and lunches another was saner in terms of switching my mindset and ingredients. It also allowed time to clean up the mess from the first batch. Allow some extra flexibility for those times when you inevitably run out of a critical item and have to go to the store. Set aside additional time to assemble drinks and snacks.

Some thru-hikers prefer to bring separate components to mix and match on the trail depending on what they feel like eating. That's a good choice for some. I'm usually too tired to think that hard after a long day of hiking and I prefer to make things as easy as possible on the trail. For me, that translates to pre-packaged meals that only require the addition of water.

Recipes for flavorful and nutritious meals that you can create efficiently (once you assemble the ingredients) are provided in Chapter 11.

These three strategies are not mutually exclusive. I often alternate homemade meals with commercial dinners and I use both home-dehydrated and bulk freeze-dried ingredients. I occasionally cook a whole meal and dehydrate it.

One important fact is that food has to be palatable to be eaten. It takes trial and error to figure out what works best but one piece of advice is to not make a wholesale change in your diet when planning a big hike. If you normally eat junk food, this is not the time to decide to go on a health kick. It's more important to be able to eat and get enough calories than to all of a sudden decide that now is the time to consume vegetables.

Freeze-dried ingredients can be purchased in bulk #10 cans

Summary

There are three basic strategies for planning food, each with pros and cons:

- Buy commercial freeze-dried meals, perhaps supplemented with additional ingredients.
- Dehydrate whole meals.
- Buy or dry separate freeze-dried or home-dehydrated ingredients to assemble meals.

Chapter 2: Know Before You Get Started

Before we dive in to food preparation there are a few things you need to know about equipment, methods, special diets and food storage.

Bear Proofing Food

Food has to fit in an approved bear-proof canister in some parks, including those in the Sierra Nevada, and may soon be required in some east coast locations. In other regions, hanging from a rope may be permitted. These methods protect your food from critters and protect the bears by preventing them from getting used to human food. In the past, bears have suffered greatly due to a lack of understanding about what drives their behavior. Problem bears get used to easy calories when they have access to human food. Unfortunately, they often end up having to be destroyed. Another successful method is to use metal food lockers, which some parks, such as Sequoia National Park, have installed in backcountry locations. Different jurisdictions have different requirements.

The most popular hard-sided bear canisters are the Bear Vault, Wild Ideas' Bearikade and Garcia Backpacker Food Cache. These are all approved for Sierra parks and forests (including Yosemite National Park, Kings Canyon National Park, Sequoia National Park and Inyo National Forest). Check Yosemite National Park, Sequoia Kings Canyon National Parks (SEKI) or other jurisdictions for current information regarding which food-protection methods are required. Inyo National Forest and some national parks allow use of another product, the soft-sided Ursack, but as of this writing, neither Yosemite nor SEKI allow Ursacks.

The biggest challenge for JMT/PCT hikers is fitting food into a canister for the stretch between Muir Trail Ranch (MTR) or Vermillion Valley Ranch (VVR) and Mt. Whitney. These are the only trail-side resupply locations in the southern Sierra section. This section can take ten days or more, depending on your pace. I have found that ten days is our max with each of us carrying a can. Others can do better, somehow getting more days' worth of calorie-dense food to fit in their can.

Once, when we hiked the High Sierra Trail, I thought I packed ten days of food for two of us in my canister. To be honest, it didn't really fit and Steve carried several Mountain House meal pouches in his pack. Luckily, Sequoia National Park has liberally sprinkled bear proof lockers throughout the wilderness so we were still able to store food legally. Unluckily for us though, we were hungry by the time we ran down the hill from the top of Whitney because we didn't really have enough food, even though we finished ahead of schedule. That was our shake-down trip before tackling the JMT so that's when I started paying more attention to the importance of food.

One important consideration is that you don't have to carry the food you're going to consume during the day in the canister. That means that on the first day that you leave your resupply location you can carry your lunch and dinner for that day outside of the canister. That helps a little, but it's still a challenge.

Garcia Backpacker Food Cache (left rear), Wild Ideas' Bearikade (right rear), Ursack (front)

Stove

There are many, many types of backcountry stoves available for purchase. There are even some do-it-yourself (DIY) designs you can make at home. Some people prefer to have a pot to simmer foods in, while others like integrated models that just boil water. The focus of this book is on foods that only need to be rehydrated, but they can certainly be simmered in a pot, if preferred.

Many modern stoves use fuel canisters that are pre-filled with liquid fuel blends, such as isobutane and propane. Some stoves can utilize a variety of types of fuel, including kerosene and white gas, in a refillable canister. The simplest, lightweight stoves use denatured alcohol. Some alternative fuel stoves use solid fuel pellets or wood (e.g. twigs).

Any stove that can boil water can be used to rehydrate food, but in certain fire-prone areas, some wilderness agencies may have restrictions on the type of stove that can be used. It's best to check for any restrictions before deciding on the type of stove to purchase.

Many foods can be rehydrated using cool or cold water, though it will take longer. Most hikers prefer hot drinks and meals, but not all.

If you are a gear junkie, you'll probably end up like us with a large collection of stoves. We mostly use the self-contained JetBoil due to its lightweight design, fuel efficiency and speed of boiling. When solo, I use an MSR Pocket Rocket and a titanium cup. Both of these stoves use isobutane-propane fuel canisters.

The JetBoil (left) and MSR Pocket Rocket stoves are two of many options. Also pictured: Green Nalgene bottle and insulated cup (left) and Toaks titanium cup (right).

Food Cozy

An insulated cozy weighs hardly anything and keeps food warm during chilly evenings. If you are familiar with a tea cozy, you can imagine what a food cozy is like. It's made of an insulated material, such as Reflectix, and is designed to hold commercial freeze-dried meals or a bag of homemade dehydrated food inside while it rehydrates. Reflectix is a reflective insulation sheet that looks like bubble wrap covered with foil. It prevents heat loss during the rehydration period so you have a hot, tasty meal at the end of the day.

This do-it-yourself Reflectix food cozy weighs 1 3/8 ounces

A food cozy can easily be made at home using Reflectix (available at home supply stores and Amazon) or a reflective windshield sunshade and duct tape. You can also purchase them. To make one, cut the insulating material in a rectangle. Make the rectangle long enough to fold over a gallon zip-top bag once. Make it wide enough to hold the gallon zip-top bag filled with food. If desired, you can leave a couple of inches on the long end so it can fold over the bag like an envelope. Apply duct tape to two sides, and you have a cozy. There are instructional videos if you search for "freezer bag cooking cozy." This is an optional item, but is useful for improving the quality of your meal. A cozy can also be made to wrap around a pot.

Freezer-Bag Cooking

Freezer-bag cooking involves rehydrating foods in a bag (or bowl or pot, if preferred) with hot water. Hot water makes food more appetizing, but the truth is that many foods will rehydrate in cool water. Though cold water is effective, it takes more time—up to several hours, depending on the type of food and ambient temperature. Thick freezer bags are strong enough to hold hot water without springing a leak, and are reusable. A food- and medical-grade product called an OpSak is even thicker.

Cajun style rice rehydrates in an OpSak

An alternative is to use the same type of bags that commercial outfits use. They look like foil pouches but they are actually made from Mylar, a clear material made from a polyester resin laminated to aluminum foil. The recipes in Chapter 11 are intended to be rehydrated in hot water, not simmered, using whatever method is desired (zip-top baggie, Mylar bag, bowl or pot). Just add warm or hot water to the bag, let it sit until the food is rehydrated and eat. Of course, simmering is just as effective and can be faster if you prefer to cook with a pot.

Rehydration Time

At sea level, pour hot water over food and allow 5-10 minutes to rehydrate. Stir or lightly knead the bag to fully distribute the liquid and repeat at the halfway mark. Test a spoonful and, if it's still crunchy, allow more time. Some instructions for commercial meals result in a meal that has too much liquid so it's prudent to add ½ or ¾ of the amount called for initially. You can add more hot water if needed. This has the added benefit of rewarming a meal that may have cooled as it rehydrates in cold mountain air. A food cozy will help retain heat (see above).

At altitude, it takes longer to rehydrate because the boiling point of water is reduced. Rehydration time approximately doubles for every 5,000 feet of elevation gain. Therefore, a meal that might take 10 minutes to rehydrate at sea level can take 40 minutes at 10,000 feet. Some foods take longer than others. Freeze-dried strawberries will rehydrate in a few minutes while dehydrated ground beef may take 15 minutes or longer, even at sea level. Here is a chart that estimates cooking time relative to sea level

Rough estimate of cooking times

- Sea level: 10 minutes
- 5,000 feet: 20 minutes
- 10,000 feet: 40 minutes
- 15,000 feet: 70 minutes
- 20,000 feet: 130 minutes

Cooking With a Pot

If you prefer to cook with a pot, simmering is just as effective for the meals presented in this book, and will open up other possibilities as well (cooking meals from scratch in the field is beyond the scope of this book).

Cooking with a pot

- To save fuel, it is recommended that you soak the food for a few minutes (5-10 minutes) before heating.

- Bring the food to a boil with the lid on.
- Simmer for 1 minute.
- Wait 10 minutes to allow food to completely rehydrate.

Re-Packaging

It's amazing how much space can be saved by repackaging commercial backpacking meals into zip-top bags. It's tempting to use freezer-bags for everything but that extra weight will add up. Many foods can be safely stored in regular baggies, which are thinner and lighter than freezer-bags. However, it is a good idea to use freezer-bags for liquid items (e.g. a bag that protects a plastic bottle of olive oil), powders and smelly items. Keep in mind that following Leave No Trace (lnt.org) principles means that all baggies and trash must be packed out.

Restricted Diets

Finding foods for backpacking can be challenging if you're on a restricted diet. Some people are on special diets out of choice, perhaps electing to be vegetarian, vegan or gluten-free, while others have medical conditions such as diabetes, high blood pressure, celiac disease or irritable bowel syndrome. The best way to avoid ingredients or additives that you don't want to eat is to create your own meals.

I am prone to migraines and try to avoid known migraine triggers. Unfortunately, this cuts out a lot of common backpacking foods such as cured meats, aged cheese and anything with nitrate/nitrites, MSG or tyramine. I have no idea which foods, if any, are true triggers for me, so it involves a bit of trial and error. My personal experience has led me to many excellent purveyors of healthy foods, and I look for sources that use the fewest additives possible.

If you're on a restricted diet, regardless of the reason, you'll find that locating minimally processed foods and/or dehydrating your own food frees you to create meals that follow the same principles you use at home. See my list of vendors in the Appendix to find some of the specialty sources that might meet your needs.

Food Purveyors

Supermarkets are the easiest place to look for food and likely the least expensive. It may take some searching to find healthy, less processed options that aren't loaded with MSG, nitrates and nitrites. They may be there, hidden on the far reaches of the shelf because they often aren't the biggest brands.

Trader Joe's is one purveyor that guarantees no MSG in any store-label food. They also have a wide variety of freeze-dried fruits, including tropical fruits, and vegetables that are made for snacking and also work well in recipes. TJ's also has many healthier varieties of canned goods that can be dehydrated at home. Instead of making beans or chili, you could purchase them, mash them up a bit and dehydrate for a quicker alternative than making everything from scratch.

REI and outdoor retailers carry a variety of freeze-dried foods, including organic foods, energy bars and hydration mixes.

Specialty items such as coconut cream powder, sour cream powder, individual condiments or ingredients for special diets can be harder to find. In many urban areas, Asian and Mexican food stores can be a good source for certain items. The bulk bins at natural food markets are a treasure trove of trail food, ranging from instant soup mixes to dehydrated bean flakes. The internet offers access to just about any food out there, including Amazon, the online retailer that seems to have everything ever made. There are many other specialized food sources listed in the Appendix, including organic, vegetarian, vegan, gluten-free, ethnic, minimally processed, preservative-free, MSG-free, etc.

Keep It Simple

Be aware that if you are very fatigued, you are not going to want to search around in camp assembling complicated, multi-part meals, so do as much as you can at home. Most of the recipes in this book involve one step (a couple of them involve a simple second step, such as mixing instant mashed potatoes). The time you spend shopping, prepping and repackaging will pay off on the trail. In Chapter 3, we'll look at some practical strategies for food planning.

Food Safety

Keeping food safe to eat is very important for long-distance hikers. The longer food is stored, the more important it is to assure that it is free from microbial contamination and will be safe to eat weeks or months after being packed in resupply boxes. This is a difficult topic to address because official recommendations from government, university and commercial product sources are fairly conservative and sometimes impractical for the thru-hiker. I believe that hikers should be aware of the guidelines from reliable sources. From this position of knowledge they are free to make their own decisions. I am not advocating unsafe practices but know that many thru-hikers choose to ignore recommendations. Each person must evaluate their own risk profile and understand the risks.

Food-borne illness, which is often due to such microbial culprits as *Salmonella, E. Coli, Listeria or Shigella,* can result in nausea, vomiting or diarrhea. It can start within hours or days of eating contaminated food. It usually resolves by itself. Sometimes symptoms can be severe and is no fun to deal with on the trail. Prevent food poisoning by adhering to accepted food-handling practices when handling, dehydrating and packaging food.

Enemies of Long Term Storage

Moisture

A moist environment allows microbial growth. Removing moisture by dehydrating or freeze-drying food combats moisture. Freeze-drying removes 98-99% of moisture. Commercial dehydrating procedures can remove 90-95% of moisture. Home dehydration can be variable with about 70% moisture removal.

Air

Air allows moisture to be re-absorbed into dried foods. Vacuum sealing in FoodSaver bags is an effective way to remove air. Another method involves using oxygen absorber packets with Mylar bags. Desiccant packets can be used in packages that will be opened and closed frequently (do not use desiccant and oxygen absorbers together). Zip-top baggies are not effective at keeping air out.

Temperature

After opening commercial packages or assembling meals, freeze to halt microbial spoilage until needed. Once you're on the trail there's not much you can do about temperature.

Fat

Rancidity, the development of unpleasant odors and tastes, is due to the oxidation of fat and oil. This is unpalatable and possibly unhealthy. The health risk is less about immediate food poisoning and more about long term effects from toxic compounds such as advanced lipid oxidation end products. Experts don't agree on how dangerous rancid food is but, regardless, it doesn't taste good. Limiting fats in home-prepared meals prevents rancidity from developing. Fats, such as olive oil, can be added to food on the trail.

Shelf Life

Packaged foods

Foods left in their original packaging will last a long time (check "use by" and "best by" dates on the package). If it's practical, don't open packages until the last minute, or until your resupply. This can be done with jerky, for example, which can be repackaged at the resupply location instead of at home weeks before.

Freeze-dried food

Because most of the moisture and oxygen has been removed, freeze-dried food has a long shelf life in unopened containers. Mountain House cans of chicken, for example, have a stated shelf-life of 30 years. What about after the can or pouch is opened? Honeyville peas (and other fruits and vegetables) have a shelf life of 12-18 months after opening. The Honeyville freeze-dried chicken label says that it can be stored in the refrigerator for one month but if not refrigerated, only one week. Pouches of freeze-dried meat can be mailed to resupply locations. They can then be added to vegetarian meals on the trail. And, of course, unopened commercial meals such as Mountain House dinners, are the safest option.

Home-dehydrated food

In general, foods dehydrated at home will have a shorter shelf life than freeze-dried due to the amount of residual moisture. Dried fruits and vegetables will keep for six to twelve months if stored in a cool, dry place. Particular care should be taken with homemade meat. Homemade jerky can last between two weeks and two months at room temperature, depending on different preparation techniques and different references. Dehydrating complete meals can be problematic if meals contain meats or oils. Oil causes rancidity. Dehydrated whole meals may only be appropriate for short term use, depending on the ingredients.

Strategies to Reduce the Risk of Spoilage

Hygiene

Washing hands before handling food is a good start. It may sound like overkill, but using medical gloves when handling food is one way to reduce microbial contamination from your hands. I bought a box of medical gloves at the pharmacy to use when I'm elbow-deep in food prep for a long hike. Wipe down countertops and keep surfaces as clean as possible.

Vacuum Seal Food

Vacuum-sealing, which removes air, helps to reduce spoilage. It does not eliminate the risk. A popular brand is FoodSaver. Another method is to use Mylar bags and oxygen absorber packets.

Freeze Food

Freezing food until needed will also reduce, but not eliminate, risk.

A winning combination is to avoid touching food with bare hands, vacuum seal food and store it in the freezer until needed.

More information can be found in the Food Safety section of Appendix 1. Links to reliable sources are provided so you can do additional research.

FoodSaver vacuum sealer (Photo by Joe Long, bit.ly/2o5D0oi)

Summary

Before you jump into recipes and food planning, review this chapter to understand a few basics:

- Be familiar with equipment choices: bear canisters, stoves, etc.
- Understand freezer-bag cooking and repackaging strategies.
- Determine how long it will take to rehydrate food.
- Know how to manage restrictive diets and where to obtain special foods.
- Appreciate the enemies of long-term storage: moisture, air and fat.

Chapter 3: What's in Your Food?

This section is about making sure you have enough calories and nutrients to sustain your backpacking activity over the weeks or months that you will be on the trail. It's a relatively deep dive. If you're not interested in the details, skip to the summary at the end of the chapter. You can always return when you want to learn more. This information is based on traditional recommendations from reliable sources, sports nutritionists, registered dieticians and government resources, with a focus on the needs of backpackers.

Hikers generally engage in relatively low-intensity exercise that lasts many hours compared to sprinters or ball players. It's not over in an hour or a day, so the challenges of staying optimally fueled over the long haul can be challenging.

Formulas for calculating calorie and protein needs are available to make planning easier. It may sound technical, but it's easy to do if you spend a few minutes plugging in your numbers. It will make a difference if you can target these data in your daily diet. However, if you're not a numbers person you might be interested in a short-cut method: weighing your food. See the section on "Calories by weight" below.

If you follow a special type of diet, it probably works well for you. Recommendations in this book may not be effective for you. Everyone has different preferences, as evidenced by the plethora of diets and recipes in the world. Dietary preferences involve trial and error, as well as some accommodation for physiologic differences. There are many ways to have a successful hike. The important thing is to do your own research, get trail experience and be sure that your food plan works for you.

Inga and Steve enjoy dinner on the John Muir Trail

Calories

The calorie, for our purposes, refers to a unit of energy that allows us to measure the energy value of food. Calories are necessary for metabolism and for use by muscles and other organs.

The question of how many calories a person needs when backpacking can be tricky. Formulas are a good starting point as long as it's understood that some will over- or under-predict your needs. The best way to confirm requirements is to gain experience. You can use the formulas for initial planning, then go backpacking and see how it goes. I've seen estimates as high as 5,000 calories per day. That may be true for some, especially for those hiking 15-20 miles a day or with a fast metabolism. Some people simply need more or less food than others, though age and level of activity has a lot to do with it. For my husband and me, 5,000 calories is much more than we need in a day. We would never be able to consume that much food. Even with fewer calories than that we used to come home with a lot of extra food.

There are a few things for thru-hikers to be aware of:

You need to eat whether you're hungry or not.

You're in it for the long-haul, not just a weekend jaunt in the woods, so you have to eat even if you're not hungry. Food is fuel and you need to treat it like medicine. If you don't have an appetite, or worse, if you are nauseated from the altitude or another reason, eat slowly and pace yourself. Eat small portions several hours apart. Some people like to get up in the morning and have a snack, then have a second breakfast a few miles down the trail. You can eat half your dinner as soon as you set up camp and warm it up to eat the second half after you've cleaned up and relaxed. You may have to experiment to find what works for you.

Your appetite will likely change over time.

A true hiker-sized appetite can kick in after the first week or so for some people. This becomes important for planning. Go lighter in calories early in the trip and add more calories to meals later on. A classic mistake is to over-pack for the first week, not eat all of the food and discard it at the first resupply. Then the "hungries" hit and hikers feel ravenous. Don't make this error in planning. If I have some dinners that are a little light in calories or volume I'll include those in the first leg of the trip. If I have some monster meals I'll put them in later resupplies. I'll look at the trail plan and have extra calories available on days when a lot of miles or big ascents are required. It doesn't hurt to have some extra treats on those days, too. I make sure to have some tried-and-true favorite meals toward the end, when we might be getting tired of our trail food.

You need to adjust your calories based on activity.

Take into consideration how far you're hiking and what the terrain is like. We usually hike about 10 miles a day, whereas PCT or AT thru-hikers could easily hike twice that. I don't need nearly the calories for a nice, flat trail (I've never seen one of those in the Sierra but they must exist somewhere!) compared to what I need huffing and puffing up Mt. Whitney. Ralph Burgess, who did the JMT in four and a half days surely needed vastly more calories per day than I did doing it in three weeks.

You need to eat throughout the day.

Your body needs energy from food at regular intervals. You may find that fats and protein are not as easily digested when you're exerting yourself. It's best to consume easily digestible carbohydrates during the day and save the bulk of fats and protein for the evening meal, though small amounts throughout the day are usually OK.

Calculating Calories

To find out how many calories you need, first calculate your basal metabolic rate (BMR) using an online BMR calculator. BMI-Calculator.net is a good one (www.bmi-calculator.net/bmr-calculator/; don't forget to type the hyphens), though many exist. This will tell you how many calories you need when you're doing nothing, just lying around breathing and not doing anything strenuous. Then use another formula, called the Harris-Benedict equation, to find out how many calories you need during varying levels of activity. Don't be intimidated. It will take less than five minutes to use the calculators that are available at BMI-Calculator.net and the application does the math.

"Go to BMI-Calculator.net to find out how many calories you need."

Here are some quick and dirty numbers for a few data points that illustrate some variations based on different factors using BMI-Calculator.net.

Calorie needs at rest (BMR):

- Female, 30 years old, 5'5", 130 lbs: BMR is 1472 calories (or roughly 1,500 calories)
- Male, 30 years old, 6'0", 200 lbs: BMR is 2022 calories (or roughly 2000 calories)

Now let's add in some backpacking activity. Using the Harris-Benedict formula, we'll take the highest level of activity (very hard exercise/sports) and multiply the above result by 1.9, which is close enough to say that you can roughly double your calories needs when you're exercising heavily. A reference from the U.S. military, *The Special Operations Forces Nutrition Guide*, expands the range of the Harris-Benedict equation with an upper limit of 2.4 as the multiplier (instead of 1.9) for "exceptional activity." This may address concerns that some hikers have expressed regarding an under-estimation of caloric needs using the Harris-Benedict formula.

HARRIS-BENEDICT MULTIPLIER	
Little to no exercise	BMR x 1.2
Light exercise 1-3 days/week	BMR x 1.375
Moderate exercise 3-5 days/week	BMR x 1.55
Hard exercise 6-7 days/week	BMR x 1.725
Very hard exercise	BMR x 1.9

U.S. MILITARY MULTIPLIER	
Very light activity	BMR x 1.3
Light activity	BMR x 1.6
Moderate activity	BMR x 1.7
Heavy activity	BMR x 2.1
Exceptional activity	BMR x 2.4

Calorie needs with strenuous activity:

- Female, 30 years old, 5'5", 130 lbs: BMR of 1472 calories x 1.9 = 2,797
- Male, 30 years old, 6'0", 200 lbs: BMR of 2022 calories x 1.9 = 3,841

It's pretty obvious that there could be a wide range of calorie expenditures captured in "very hard exercise." Hard exercise for two hours will expend a lot fewer calories than 6 or 8 hours so formulas aren't perfect. For the examples below I'll use 1.9, the highest level of the standard Harris-Benedict equation. Perhaps you'll find an example that is similar to you.

Calorie needs with strenuous activity (more examples using 1.9 as the multiplier):

FEMALE	CALORIES/DAY
Female, 20, 5'0", 110 lbs	2509 calories
Female, 30, 5'5", 130 lbs	2631 calories
Female, 50, 5'8", 130 lbs	2479 calories
Female, 50, 5'8", 200 lbs	3057 calories
Female, 65, 5'6", 140 lbs	2400 calories

MALE	CALORIES/DAY
Male, 20, 5'8', 180 lbs	3638 calories
Male, 30, 6'0", 200 lbs	3841 calories
Male, 40, 6'4", 250 lbs	4400 calories
Male, 50, 6'2", 230 lbs	3986 calories
Male, 65, 5'10", 175 lbs	3045 calories

We can see that 2500-3000 calories are a good starting point for women, while men may need a minimum of 3000-4500 calories per day. If using a higher multiplier the calorie totals will be even greater.

I found that 1280 calories meet my BMR needs and my requirement for strenuous activity is 2,430 calories. My husband's calorie needs for strenuous activity is 2,900. Formulas don't work for everyone, but in our case we found that it's a pretty good estimate of our needs. Using these numbers as a guide I find that we bring home less excess food at the end of a trip than we used to.

Calories by Weight

A quick and dirty way to estimate calories is to weigh your food. This sounds daunting if you weigh each item. An easy way to do this is to assemble the food allotted for one person for one day, including snacks, and weigh the bundle. Another method is to assemble all of the food for a trip and weigh it. Divide by the number of days of the trip and the number of people to obtain the food weight per person for one day.

"A good rule of thumb is to pack 1.5-2.5 pounds of food per day."

The usual goal adopted by some long-distance through hikers is around 1.5 to 2.5 pounds per person per day, which will provide approximately 2,500-4,500 calories per day. Size, weight and metabolism varies by individual, so some petite hikers might be able to get away with less than 1.5 pounds per day, while tall, muscular trekkers might need more than 2.5 pounds per day.

Many long distance hikers attempt to achieve about 125 calories per ounce when evaluating food choices to target relatively calorie-dense foods. Since carbohydrates and protein have 4 calories per gram, while fats have 9 calories per gram, the higher the fat content the greater the caloric density. Olive oil or other fats contain a whopping 250 calories per ounce! It's too bad most people can't stomach a diet of pure fat. "Wet" food, such as fresh fruit, contains less than 100 calories per ounce and is not a good choice for backpacking.

"Use calorie-dense foods of around 125 calories per ounce."

Some well-known long-distance hikers come in at either end of the spectrum. Ray Jardine, author of the book, *Trail Life: Ray Jardine's Lightweight Backpacking*, recommends 2.5 pounds per day while Andrew Skurka, author of *The Ultimate Hiker's Gear Guide: Tools and Techniques to Hit the Trail* uses 1.5 pounds per day (or less) as his standard. Justin Lichter (aka "Trauma"), author of *Trail Tested: A Thru-Hiker's Guide to Ultralight Hiking and Backpacking*, plays it safe with a range of 1.5 to 2.5 pounds per day with foods that have around 125 calories per ounce. In the classic reference book, *Mountaineering, The Freedom of the Hills*, the recommendation is 2 pounds per day. This assumes typical backpacker food comprised of a significant amount of dehydrated food that has been repackaged. This will reduce water and packaging weight. Though this method has obvious drawbacks in terms of accuracy, it is a surprisingly effective surrogate to use instead of complex formulas.

Carbohydrates

When I'm at home I prefer to eat whole foods as much as possible, but I have my weaknesses like everyone else. Processed foods range from the most basic modification necessary to make foods edible, such as mechanically grinding wheat into flour, to fantastic marvels of modern science that renders food unrecognizable with unpronounceable ingredients. Entire books have been written on the subject of whether processed foods are healthy or not. Suffice to say that I generally prefer less processed foods, however, don't take my potato chips away—especially on a zero day (a day with zero miles hiked)! I've learned through trial and error that I need a slightly different diet on the trail compared to what I eat at home. I use the same kinds of grains and starches in my trail meals—such as quinoa, rice and potatoes—that I consume at home, but I also eat a lot more sweets when I'm actively hiking. I've found that gourmet jelly beans, lemon drops and licorice bits are appealing, digestible and provide reliable bursts of energy that I need throughout the day. I also use protein bars and nuts in addition to a proper lunch break. Others might find my choices unpalatable. It takes experience to know what will work for you.

Carbohydrates are the main form of fuel for most athletes, including hikers. They take many forms, including bread, pasta, grains, fruits, vegetables and sweets. Carbohydrates are broken down into sugars (glucose) to provide fuel for muscles and the brain. These sugars and starches are important in maintaining energy. Glucose that is not immediately used is stored as glycogen in muscles and the liver.

During exercise, glycogen is released from its storage depot in the muscles and liver. The body can store enough glycogen to provide about 1,600 calories at a time. This can last anywhere from one to three hours during moderate to heavy exercise. The liver can supply a small amount of glycogen but not as much as muscles. When muscle glycogen has been depleted, muscle fibers can't contract. The resulting weakness and fatigue can lead to a condition that athletes often refer to as "hitting the wall," where they can't continue. Liver glycogen feeds the brain, so when those stores are used up symptoms of low blood sugar can develop. These symptoms, which can include irritability, impaired vision, balance issues, dizziness and inability to focus, are collectively known as "bonking."

Muscles will use glucose from the blood instead of using up their glycogen. If there is a steady supply of blood glucose, it can prevent fatigue. Consuming small quantities of a variety of sugars that are easily absorbed over time allows the body to gradually absorb the sugar for ready consumption by the muscles. Sports drinks usually contain a mixture of different sugars for this reason.

"The Glycemic Index ranks the ability of carbohydrates to raise blood sugar."

Some carbs are absorbed quickly while others take more time. The Glycemic Index ranks the ability of carbs to raise blood sugar (see list of Glycemic Index foods in Appendix 5 and a few examples below). What type of carbohydrate is best depends on the time of day. At breakfast and lunch you want carbohydrates that will give you immediate energy as most people start hiking right after breakfast and right through the day. Breakfast might consist of instant oatmeal with honey and nuts while lunch could be a tortilla with rice and beans. If you need quick energy to power you up a steep mountain, you'll need a gel, sports drink or candy bar that has a high glycemic index for immediate use. At dinner you can choose carbohydrates that have a lower glycemic index, which often include more nutrient-rich foods such as beans, whole grains and vegetables. These can be digested over a longer period of time as you sleep.

Examples of Low Glycemic Index Foods:

- Nuts and seeds
- Beans
- Brown rice

- Peanut butter
- Fruits and vegetables
- Milk
- Chocolate

Examples of High Glycemic Index Foods

- Dry cereals
- Instant oatmeal
- Potato
- White rice
- White bread
- Gatorade

Steve downs a mid-morning snack

It is generally recommended to get a little more than half (50-70%) of total calories from carbohydrates. A good rule of thumb is to get 30-60 grams of carbohydrate per hour during exercise lasting more than 90 minutes. Try to get 1-1.5 grams of carbohydrate per kilogram of body weight within 30 minutes of finishing your hike for the day. If you're looking for a formula, calculate 3.4-4.5 grams of carbohydrate per pound of body weight (8-10 grams per kilogram). A good way to plan is to calculate protein and fat first, then get the balance of calories from carbohydrates.

Protein

I never worried about anything except calories when I did shorter trips, but on my first hike that lasted more than a week I found our diet was inadequate. I was hungry! And I wasn't craving plain ol' calories. I wanted meat, and a lot of it. After eight days on the High Sierra Trail I found myself running, not walking, to Whitney Portal for their legendary hamburgers. We planned to camp one additional night along the trail but, as day hikers were coming up, I interrogated each one about the food that was available at the Whitney Portal Store. The stories were tantalizing. Eggs, pancakes, French fries, hamburgers, even real lettuce and tomato slices. It was all too much for me and after I wiped the drool off my face, I turned to Steve and said, "I can't take it. I have to have a hamburger *tonight*." And I don't even like hamburgers that much.

I wondered if our diet had enough protein. When I calculated our protein needs I found that we were pretty light. Most Americans get much more protein than they need, but the typical backpacking diet is heavy in carbohydrates. Protein can be lacking.

Though you don't need protein for immediate energy (carbs take care of that), you do need protein to build and repair all that muscle that you're tearing down and rebuilding. Proteins are broken into amino acids through digestion. After that, they are used to build a body protein or, if not needed for that purpose, can be converted into glucose to be used for energy, or fat for storage. This conversion process requires nitrogen to be stripped away, which may be excreted as urea or ammonia in urine. Animal proteins contain all the necessary amino acids to create human protein while plant sources have gaps in their composition, with the exception of soy, quinoa, hempseed and buckwheat. Vegetarians and vegans often look for food combinations that provide complete proteins. It used to be thought that complementary proteins had to be eaten together. Research has shown that that is not the case and as long as a variety of foods are eaten throughout the day vegetarians and vegans will not suffer from a lack of protein. Common combinations that assure a complete protein intake are grains with legumes or milk products, or legumes with nuts or seeds.

Protein cannot be absorbed rapidly, so it is best to consume small amounts at every meal, along with carbohydrates and fat. Muscle repair may continue for 24-48 hours, which, for the long distance hiker means that it's a continuous process. When carbohydrate stores are low, muscle tissue may burn amino acids for energy. When carbohydrate levels are adequate, adding protein during exertion doesn't improve performance. However, during the recovery period it is possible that muscle soreness may be lessened if protein is consumed along with carbohydrates.

Aim for 15-25% of total calories in protein. According to the Institute of Medicine, 0.36 grams of protein per pound of body weight per day (0.8 g/kg/day) is the recommended amount for most people. However, many sports organizations recommend higher amounts ranging from 0.45-0.9 grams per pound per day (1-2 g/kg/day), though there is no consensus. There is a limit to how much our bodies can use. We can't process more than 4.5-5.5 grams per pound (2-2.5 grams/kg) efficiently. If your sweat smells like ammonia it could be a sign of excessive protein, but this is not a problem most long-distance hikers have. Below are some calculations (using the lower and upper amounts recommended by sports authorities, 0.45 and 0.9 grams per pound, with some rounding).

"Many sports nutrition experts recommend 0.45-0.9 grams of protein per pound of body weight per day during periods of exertion."

I found that, at 132 lbs, I needed about 60 grams of protein a day. In the field this resulted in better stamina and less hunger over the long haul. Here is the calculation:

- 132 lbs x 0.45 grams=60 grams/day of protein
- 132 lbs x 0.9 grams=120 grams/day of protein

The average 154 lb (70 kg) person would need 70 grams of protein per day.

- 154 lbs x 0.45 grams=70 grams/day of protein
- 154 lbs x 0.9 grams= 140 grams/day of protein

A 200 lb (90 kg) individual would need 90 grams of protein per day.

- 200 lbs x 0.45 grams=90 grams/day of protein
- 200 lbs x 0.9 grams= 180 grams/day of protein

Calculate your protein needs:

Lower end: ______ pounds x 0.45 grams = ______ grams/day of protein

Upper end: ______ pounds x 0.9 grams = ______ grams/day of protein

I did a quick tally of our usual backpacking diet and found that it only contained about 40 grams of protein. For example, Mountain House dinners only have 6-14 grams of protein per serving. If you eat two servings by yourself you'd get 12-28 grams. That's still pretty light on protein. If you're eating cereal for breakfast you'll need to pay particular attention to lunches and snacks to boost your protein, or add protein in other ways. I wasn't a slave to these numbers but I managed to get our protein content to 60-70 grams per day by adding seeds, nuts, cheese, legumes and extra freeze-dried meats to our meals.

The quickest way for me to add a chunk of protein was by adding one high-protein energy bar to my diet each day. The Clif Builder Bars I used contained 20 grams of protein. In one fell swoop I took care of a third of my protein needs with one small item. I tested some bars with 30 grams but didn't find them as palatable. I brought some of the 30-gram bars anyway for the third week, figuring that I'd need it most then. They were fine. It didn't matter if I loved them or not. I ate them every day. I'd eat a quarter at mid-morning, a quarter in the afternoon and the rest when we were setting up camp. Some days I was very hungry in the morning and would eat the whole bar before lunch. Some people choose to supplement their protein intake with protein powders. There are lots of ways to add protein so you can figure out what works for you.

Fats

Since so much backpacking food is dried or processed in some way, fats are limited. I use olive oil to add fat into our diet on the trail to provide flavor and calories. It's the one heavy liquid that I bring (aside from water), adding it to the dinner meal while it is rehydrating. I use between 1 teaspoon and 1 tablespoon per serving. At lunch I have some cheese, usually string cheese. At breakfast I get a small amount of fat in my whole milk powder. I usually have some nuts for snacking, which also provides some fat.

Fats play an important role in providing fuel, in addition to carbohydrates and protein. Fat makes food taste better. It takes longer for fat to leave your stomach so it keeps you feeling full longer, which can be more satisfying. Fat in food is necessary for the production of hormones and the absorption of nutrients. Foods that contain fat can help you stay warm as your body works to metabolize it. An evening dollop of peanut butter can help you sleep better in cold temperatures.

Fat sources on the trail are heavy but they pack a punch, providing 9 calories per gram rather than the 4 calories per gram that carbs and protein contain. It's best to spread your fat intake throughout the day so you're not consuming it all at once. Try to incorporate 15-25% of daily calories in fat sources. One way to approach balancing your nutrients is to determine how much fat, which is heavy and often bulky, you can allocate to each day. Healthy sources of fat in a backpacking diet include olive oil, ghee (clarified butter), coconut oil, cheese, dark chocolate, nuts, peanut butter (the real thing, not the powder), nut spreads, chia seeds and flax seeds.

Fat takes a long time to digest, which is why it makes us feel full longer. One downside to fat is that it can be harder to digest during exercise, at high altitude or in excessive temperatures. It's best to add fat to the evening meal to allow digestion to occur overnight. A large amount of fat may interfere with performance during the day, though small amounts can prevent hunger.

Vitamins

The typical backcountry diet makes some tradeoffs when it comes to vitamins. Fresh foods are often lacking. The long-term storage and processing of foods to make them appropriate for backpacking often means that vitamin levels can be variable. Eating a variety of foods and including dried vegetables and fruits can assure an adequate vitamin intake. If you're bringing commercial freeze-dried foods they may be enhanced with supplemental vitamins. For trips of a month or less, if you're healthy and eat a varied diet, you're not likely to develop a vitamin deficiency. For longer thru-hikes, town visits offer an opportunity to consume fresh fruits and vegetables. It doesn't hurt to take a few vitamin supplements but it's probably not necessary.

Water

Water is essential for survival. We humans can last weeks without food but only days without water. Water needs vary with the amount of exertion, temperature, humidity, altitude and other factors. A good starting point is 3-6 quarts (2.8-5.6 liters) a day in moderate temperatures (75 F), perhaps more. The Institute of Medicine has established nearly a gallon (3.7 liters) a day as the standard for adult men. Water losses increase at high altitude. In hot desert conditions the requirement could more than double.

Athletes and hikers are used to hearing that if you're thirsty, you're already dehydrated. That has been debunked. As athletes got used to slugging large quantities of water, another deadly problem emerged: hyponatremia (low sodium). This condition occurs when there is less sodium in the blood than needed as a result of dilution from too much water. Currently, the Wilderness Medical Society Practice Guidelines for Treatment of Exercise-Associated Hyponatremia recommend, "drinking to thirst and specifically avoiding excessively high fluid intake."

Inga is staying hydrated

Electrolytes

Electrolytes are another important component of the backpacking diet. Sodium is the main electrolyte lost in sweat, along with potassium and several others. The American Heart Association recommends no more than 2,300 milligrams of sodium (about 1 teaspoon of salt) a day. However, that does not take into consideration that a hiker who sweats a lot can lose between 460-1840 mg of sodium in one liter of sweat. Many people are surprised at how much sodium is in commercial freeze-dried meals, but many hikers need the sodium replenishment. If you crave salt, go ahead and salt your food. You probably need it.

Here are the approximate amounts of sodium in a given amount of table salt:

SALT	SODIUM (mg)
1/8 teaspoon	287
1/4 teaspoon	575
1/2 teaspoon	1,150
3/4 teaspoon	1,725
1 teaspoon	2,300

Sodium and potassium work together to regulate fluid balance. Potassium also plays a role in transporting glucose to muscles and storing glycogen. Hydration powder mixes, which usually contain several different electrolytes, are widely available at sporting goods stores. These electrolyte solutions are a convenient way to replace electrolytes while hiking, but it's not the only way. Energy bars, salted nuts, trail mix (such as raisins, nuts and chocolate) and other foods can also be good sources of electrolytes. If you take short rest breaks, it's a good idea to drink some fluid and eat a snack to provide all the components discussed in this chapter. If you find that your appetite is affected by the strenuous exertion or effects of altitude, you may find that electrolyte drink mixes are an easy and palatable way to consume calories and electrolytes. Electrolyte replacement products can be expensive. You can make your own mix using the following recipe:

Oral Rehydration Mix:

8 teaspoon sugar
1 teaspoon salt
1 teaspoon potassium, found in salt-substitute (optional)

Mix with 1 liter of water. Flavored drink powder, such as lemonade powder, can be added to improve the taste.

Gu Brew is one of many brands of electrolyte drink powders

Fiber

Fiber, which can't be digested, isn't something that is often discussed among hikers. However, some people suffer from the effects of not having enough fiber in their backpacking diet in the form of constipation. Packaged trail meals may contain much less fiber than the average hiker is used to getting. Fiber keeps the intestinal tract moving and can help regulate bowel movements. It also plays a role in slowing down digestion. This can be good or bad for the hiker. You don't want to consume a lot of fiber right before a big ascent, but fiber consumed at the end of the day can be helpful. It can keep you feeling full longer and slow the absorption of nutrients to a pace where they may be able to be better utilized by the body. It's best to consume fiber within foods. However, if you suffer from a lack of fiber, a couple of psyllium capsules (Metamucil or generic brand) or some unprocessed what bran can make or break a trip. The CDC recommends 14 grams of fiber for every 1,000 calories you consume. See "Fiber Content of Foods in Common Portions" (bit.ly/2oX6pQF) by Harvard University Health Services.

Timing is Everything

In the morning, take in carbohydrates, preferably of a high-glycemic nature, so your body can gain quick energy, sparing muscle glycogen. Examples are instant oatmeal, instant grits, breakfast cereal or bread. Add raisins, brown sugar, peanut butter and milk.

Between breakfast and lunch, continue to consume high-glycemic carbs such as energy gels, sports drinks, even candy such as jelly beans. Add medium- and low-glycemic carbohydrates such as nuts, energy bars and raisins.

At lunch, eat a mixed meal that contains both high and low glycemic carbohydrates along with a small amount of protein and fat. Take the time to fully rehydrate as well.

In the afternoon, eat the same types of foods as the morning snacks to replenish needed energy.

Within 30-45 minutes of finishing for the day, consume more high-glycemic carbohydrates to aid in recovery. Muscles store glycogen most efficiently within two hours of exercise, but the rate drops over time. Enzymes and hormones work together to speed glucose into your bloodstream and convert it to glycogen. It can take 24 hours to fully replenish glycogen but if you're going to hike again the next day you don't have that much time. Aim for consuming 1-1.5 grams of carbohydrate per kilogram of body weight as soon as possible after finishing your hike for the day. For a 70 kg person that could include a tortilla (26 grams) with 2 tablespoon peanut butter (6 grams), 1 tablespoon jam (14 grams) and 1.5 ounce raisins (34 grams). You can also choose from 1 ounce cashews (9 grams), recovery sports drink powder (50 grams, varies by brand), granola bar (18-40 grams, depending on brand), hot chocolate with milk (30 grams), or a Fig Newton (11 grams per cookie).

In the evening, eat low-glycemic carbohydrates as part of a mixed meal with protein and fat. These foods take longer to digest and your body will have time to process the food overnight. Examples of low-glycemic foods include beans, barley, peanuts.

Compare and Contrast Two Meals

Let's take an example of a meal plan for one day that consists of foods that ready-made or easy to assemble.

Meal #1

Breakfast: 2 packages instant oatmeal and 1 tablespoon powdered milk

Morning snacks: granola bar and 1 ounce (28) peanut M&M's

Lunch: 1.5 ounce ramen

Afternoon snacks: Snickers bar and 1 ounce (18) cashews

Dinner: Mountain House Spaghetti with Meat Sauce (1/2 package), 1 package hot chocolate mix, 1 tablespoon full-fat powdered milk, 1 ounce dark chocolate

MEAL #1 NUTRIENTS

- **Calories 1921**
- **Carbohydrate 233 g**
- **Protein 55 g**
- **Fat 81 g**
- **Sodium 3047 mg**

Now let's look at a meal that consists of some strategic additions to improve calories and nutrition.

Meal #2

Breakfast: 2 packages instant oatmeal, 1 tablespoon full-fat powdered milk, 1 tablespoon chopped hazelnuts, 1 tablespoon raisins, 1 tablespoon brown sugar, 1 teaspoon roasted flax seeds, 1 teaspoon chia seeds

Morning snacks: 1.4 ounce (37) gourmet jelly beans, 1 Clif Builder Bar, 1 ounce (28) Peanut M&M's, 24 grams hydration powder mix

Lunch: 1 tortilla, 1/2 cup dehydrated black bean flakes, 1/8 cup freeze-dried brown rice, 1 tablespoon sunflower seeds (unsalted), 1 string cheese, 4 Tanka Bites

Afternoon snacks: 1.4 ounce (37) gourmet jelly beans, 1/2 Nature Valley granola bar, 1 ounce (18) cashews

Recovery snack: 50 grams recovery powder mix

Dinner: Italian Sausage and Orzo (see recipe in Chapter 11), 1 package hot chocolate mix, 1 tablespoon full-fat powdered milk, 2 ounces dark chocolate

MEAL #2 NUTRIENTS

- **Calories 3688**
- **Carbohydrate 523 g**
- **Protein 126 g**
- **Fat 197 g**
- **Sodium 3343 mg**

You can see that with a little forethought and planning, meals can be created that contain more calories and protein with lower sodium.

COMPARISON OF TWO MEALS	
Meal #1	**Meal #2**
Calories 1921	Calories 3688
Carbohydrate 233 g	Carbohydrate 523 g
Protein 55 g	Protein 126 g
Fat 81 g	Fat 197 g
Sodium 3047 mg	Sodium 3343 mg

Meal #2 has an improved nutrition profile for backpacker's needs compared to Meal #1. If more calories are desired, the dinner in Meal #2 could be increased to two servings, which would bring the calorie count for the day to about 4,500. The calorie and nutrition breakdown is provided in The Hungry Spork Data Sheets (bit.ly/HungrySporkDataSheets).

Summary

- Estimate your calorie needs using the formulas provided. First calculate the number of calories needed at rest, then double that amount to account for strenuous activity. I found that my calorie needs for strenuous activity was about 2,500 calories while my husband's was about 3,000.
- A quick and dirty way to estimate calories is by weighing food, aiming for 1.5 to 2.5 pounds of food per person per day of calorie-dense food (around 125 calories per ounce).

- Carbohydrates will take care of themselves in the typical backpacking diet.
- Do another calculation to figure out your protein needs. A good starting point is 60-70 grams per day.
- Add some fat with such foods as olive oil, coconut oil or peanut butter.
- Don't worry about vitamins for trips of a month or less. For a longer trip, eat a varied diet to assure that you're getting adequate vitamins.
- Make sure you have adequate hydration, but there is no need to overdo it.
- Consume electrolytes in food or sports drinks throughout the day.

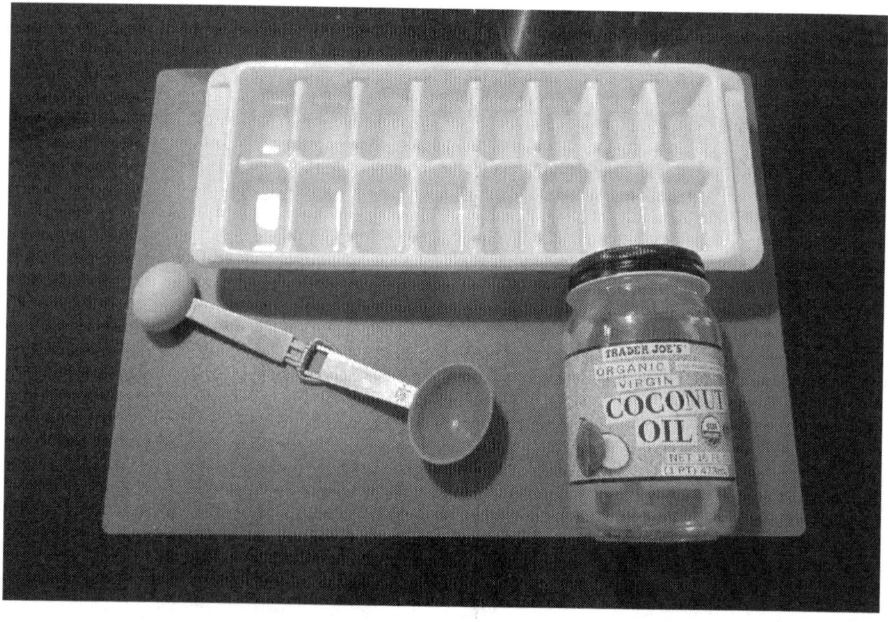

Individual servings of coconut oil (warm the coconut oil, pour into ice cube tray, refrigerate, store in pill pouch)

Chapter 4: Mapping Out Your Plan

The first step is to create a detailed meal plan. Whether you're dehydrating your own victuals, purchasing packaged meals or assembling them from dry ingredients, make a list, especially for dinners.

"See the *Six Week Plan* below for step-by-step instructions for assembling your own meals for a month-long trek."

To be clear, "six weeks" refers to the planning/prep phase, not the length of the trek. This includes one day each week for the actual prep and a few hours on other days for planning and running errands to get last-minute items. The plan can be condensed if you're purchasing meals or expanded if you're dehydrating your own. Long distance hikes of five or six months will require more lead time. People often start planning six to nine months in advance of hiking long trails such as the PCT or AT. Turn the *Six Week Plan* into a *Six Month Plan* for longer hikes.

Start prepping for a 30-day trip early but not too early. If you start packaging foods more than six to 12 months before your trip you run the risk of food going bad unless you have been meticulous in preparation and handling.

Here are some things to think about based on the three food strategies outlined in Chapter 1.

- If you're buying commercial freeze-dried meals you can start purchasing commercial freeze-dried meals as early as you want—they retain their freshness for years in their original, unopened containers. Start organizing your meals two-to-four weeks before the mail date for your resupply locations if you're buying.
- If you're dehydrating your own whole meals or most of the ingredients, start several months ahead of time. Use freezer bags or vacuum-seal the food. Vacuum-sealing is not mandatory but if you're preparing food months in advance, removing as much air as possible can maintain quality.
- If you're assembling your own meals, start six weeks (or more) ahead of time. You may only need three to five solid days of prep time after you have your ingredients but starting early alleviates some pressure in case you run out of key ingredients and have to buy or dry more. Of course, some people could accomplish this the night before. They won't be reading this book. They'll be sitting in a heap at 2 a.m., posting harried photos to Facebook as they weep!
- Tackle assembling different meals separately. See the following chapters for inspiration. Package all of your breakfasts in one sitting, then lunches, then dinners, then snacks and beverages. This will reduce your feeling of insanity about embarking on this crazy venture.

Some people, like Sarah, get very creative with planning (Photo by Sarah Kettles)

There are a few things to be aware of before you dive in to the food preparation. Since you'll be developing your plan in Week 1, most of these tips apply to Week 2 and beyond when you'll be assembling your meals.

Gather Your Supplies

Before you get started, gather your supplies. In addition to zip-top bags, make sure you have any bulk containers and all of the food components that you need.

For the zip-top bags, it's tricky to decide which can be regular thickness versus freezer thickness. In this section we're talking about the final packaging of food for the trip and for resupply containers. If all the bags are freezer thickness you'd be surprised how fast the weight and volume adds up. I generally use the thinner bags for most items. I use freezer bags for liquids stored in a plastic bottle, such as olive oil, that could cause a significant mess if the bottle broke. Most of the time I repackage everything, even items that come in their own zip top bag from the manufacturer, as those bags are often very thick and heavy. One exception is for foods that are best left in their original packaging. These include fresh items that still have a long enough shelf life to be practical for backpacking, such as tortillas and cheese.

Many of us hate how much plastic we use when backpacking and some choose to package large quantities of food in big bags to portion out on the trail. I can't do that. I need to know I have each meal accounted for. It only took one trip where I miscalculated and was short two meals to drive home the importance of basic math. Somehow on that trip to Desolation Wilderness, when I counted our meals I neglected to take into consideration the last day. We had a lengthy hike out and compounded the problem by not having enough water. We were two hot, hungry and thirsty hikers by the end. I have now become meticulous in my planning because that wasn't pretty.

Pill-pouches are handy for storing small quantities of spices and condiments. Use a permanent marker to label your food.

Wash Your Hands

Wash your hands with soap and water before handling food. Wipe down countertops, too.

Handle Food Carefully

If you're transferring food from its original container to a zip-top baggie, pour from one to the other rather than reaching in and grabbing it with your fingers. Use gloves to prevent contamination from your skin.

When you are combining ingredients make sure they are all completely dry. If you have some foods that are in doubt, such as fruit leathers that aren't completely dry, package separately. That way, if one item develops mold, it won't contaminate the whole meal.

Clear a Large Space

If you have the space in your home, cordon off an area that you can set up to organize your meals. I used a long wall in our dining room where I laid out individual meals so I could count them, and then put them in boxes, one for each week. When I had everything 100% ready I transferred them to the mailing containers for our resupply drops. It was a mess for a while, and visitors marveled at our quirkiness as they sampled freeze-dried sausage and Tang crystals.

Count and Recount

Count and recount your meals. I went for triple-redundancy, plotting out meals on a spreadsheet, counting total meals and laying out pieces of paper that designated each day. After I packaged all my breakfasts, for example, I went to the wall (no, I didn't bang my head against it) and placed one breakfast on each piece of paper (Day 1, Day 2, Day 3, etc.). I had separate sections labeled for our zero days. I did the same thing when I prepared lunches and dinners.

It's easy to count if you lay it all out like Valerie did; also note the Bear Vault in the back (Photo by Valerie Gould Eaton)

SIX WEEK PLAN

Week 1-Geek Out with a Spreadsheet

Monday: Create a chart on a spreadsheet or use old-fashioned paper and pencil, especially for dinners. Don't underestimate this stage of the planning. Some people have reported that they spent 12-30 hours just on the spreadsheet for the JMT. On this day, focus on setting up the chart. If you have a detailed trip plan, pull it out and note the days when you will have long mileage and/or steep ascents and designate your highest calorie meals for those days. If you're inclined to dig into the numbers, include a column for calorie counts.

Tuesday: Do at least a rough nutrition breakdown for a typical day, including grams of protein and perhaps carbohydrates, fats and sodium in the foods you normally eat when backpacking. Some people go wild and create a detailed analysis of all food for each day, but it's not necessary. Start with one average day.

Wednesday: Check resupply websites and know what type of container they will accept (e.g. cardboard box or plastic five-gallon bucket), print any needed paperwork and pay any required fees. Print information about needed lead times for mailing and mark important mailing dates on your calendar. Purchase needed mailing supplies such as mailing boxes, bucket and packing tape. See Chapter 14 for more information on resupply.

Thursday: Start a list of breakfast and lunch foods (see Chapter 5 and 6). I find that our breakfasts and lunches are similar each day and I vary these by changing the toppings. Therefore I don't always need a detailed chart for those meals. I can get my assembly line going and drop different toppings into the bags.

Friday: Go to the store and get repackaging and mailing supplies. See sample shopping list below.

Saturday: Spend a good amount of time coming up with a list of dinners (See Chapter 7 and 11). If you're going to purchase commercial freeze-dried food, spend some time looking at the choices online and identify the ones that sound appealing. If you're assembling or dehydrating your own meals (hopefully this is more than six weeks before your trip), look at recipes and decide which ones you like. Week 4 will be the focus for dinners but if you need specialty items or to dehydrate food, don't wait until the last minute to procure them.

I use a menu plan for dinners so I don't end up with three of the same meals in a row at the end. We found that we enjoyed scrutinizing the laminated menu I made to see what was coming up when we were on the trail.

My dinner chart contains the name of the meal, the basic components and a reminder to add olive oil, which I tend to forget. I include the main ingredients so I can be sure I'm varying the meat and grain so we don't get bored. Below is an example for one day. Repeat once for a four-week trip, twice for a six week trip and so on. Follow this link to The Hungry Spork Data Sheets (bit.ly/HungrySporkDataSheets), where I have a sample menu for 14 days. Within the 14-day menu, each dinner is unique. Though there is some repetition of breakfasts and lunches, endless variations can be used for toppings to mix things up.

DAY	BREAKFAST	LUNCH	DINNER	DESSERT
1	Oatmeal with varied toppings	Tortilla & black beans	Simple Healthy Ramen	Milk chocolate bar
2	Granola with varied toppings	Crackers & hummus	BBQ Chicken with Mashed Potatoes	Dark chocolate bar
3	Grits with varied toppings	Tortilla & peanut but	Moroccan Couscous with Lamb	Caramel chocolate bar
4	Muesli with varied toppings	Crackers & salami	Italian Sausage and Orzo Pasta	Raspberry chocolate bar
5	Cream of wheat with varied toppings	Tortilla & tuna	Mexican Black Bean and Quinoa Wrap	Orange chocolate bar
6	Quinoa with varied toppings	Ramen & veggies	Chinese Cashew Chicken Noodles	Hazelnut chocolate bar
7	Freeze-dried scrambled eggs & bacon	Tortilla & pinto beans	Cajun Chicken, Sausage and Rice	Angel food cake
8	Oatmeal with varied toppings	Tortilla & tabbouleh	Indonesian Chicken Noodles	Milk chocolate bar
9	Granola with varied toppings	Tortilla & salmon	Beef Stew with Mashed Sweet Potato	Dark chocolate bar
10	Grits with varied toppings	Tortilla & lentils	Thai Curry Chicken and Rice	Caramel chocolate bar
11	Muesli with varied toppings	Crackers & hummus	Hearty Grits with Sausage and Veggies	Raspberry chocolate bar
12	Cream of rye with varied toppings	Tortilla & red beans	Indian Chicken, Lentils and Quinoa	Orange chocolate bar
13	Quinoa flakes with varied toppings	Tortilla & peanut but	Italian Chicken and Farro	Hazelnut chocolate bar
14	Freeze-dried biscuits and gravy	Rice ramen & veggies	Moroccan Tabbouleh with Beef	Angel food cake

I create the chart in a spreadsheet, then print and cut to size. To protect the sheet, I cover one or both sides with wide strips of clear packing tape. This creates a crude form of lamination so it doesn't fall apart. It goes in the bear canister so either of us can identify the dinner for the day and get it started.

Sunday: Make a list of drinks and snacks (See Chapter 8 and 9). I've listed a variety of snacks in the spreadsheet but most people pick a few foods they like, rather than having different snacks each day. It's extremely common, verging on universal, for people to report that they hate their energy bars after a while, so I strongly recommend buying a variety of brands and flavors.

I have included several different spreadsheets in The Hungry Spork Data Sheets (bit.ly/HungrySporkDataSheets), including a master list of common foods with a complete nutrition breakdown, sample daily menus with different calorie counts, 14-day variations for breakfasts, lunches and dinners, and a sample 14-day plan with breakfast, lunch, dinner, snacks and drinks.

Week 1 sample shopping list (food packaging and mailing supplies)

- Indelible marker for labeling food bags
- Zip-top bags: at least one box of each size to start, more for a multi-month hike
  - Pill-pouch bags
  - Snack size storage bags
  - Sandwich size storage bags
  - Quart size freezer bags
  - Gallon size freezer bags
- Kitchen gloves for handling food
- Rubber bands (if desired to bundle foods together)
- Bags for rehydrating (e.g. freezer-bag, Opsak, mylar bag)

- Small plastic, leak-proof jars for liquid items
- Mailing boxes
- Five-gallon bucket with lid, if required (hardware store)
- Packing tape

Making a mess in the kitchen prepping breakfast

Week 2: Breakfast Focus

- Monday: Assess what you need for breakfasts and make a list of needed items to purchase, including cereals, toppings, eggs, coffee or tea and powdered milk. Snack size baggies work well for individual servings of cereal with toppings. Allow a couple of hours unless you have a tidy spreadsheet from your planning stage that has a list of foods you need.
- Tuesday: Go to the store and purchase needed items or order online with 2-day delivery.

- Saturday: Create an assembly line and package breakfasts for trip, varying the ingredients and following your menu plan. Wash hands and use kitchen gloves to prevent contamination of food. Allow a full day for this task for a month-long trip.
- Put all the breakfasts aside.

Week 2 sample shopping list:

- Instant oatmeal packets
- Granola
- Muesli
- Freeze-dried fruit
- Seeds and nuts
- Freeze-dried eggs
- Starbucks Via coffee packets
- Tea
- Powdered whole milk

Breakfast prep

Week 3: Lunch Focus

- Monday: Assess your supplies and purchase needed lunch items. If you are planning to use tortillas, cheese or other perishable items, don't purchase these until the last minute to ensure freshness. Start a list of "last minute items" that you will purchase a day or so before mailing. Allow a couple of hours to get your shopping list together.
- Tuesday: Go to the store and get needed items.
- Saturday: Create an assembly line and package lunch items. Allow a full day for this task for a month-long trip.

Week 3 sample shopping list

- Dehydrated bean mix
- Peanut butter
- Jelly or honey packets
- Dehydrated hummus
- Tuna packets
- Ramen
- Crackers
- Condiment packets
- Tortillas (put on the "last minute" list)
- Cheese (put on the "last minute" list)
- Salami or other cured meat (put on the "last minute" list)

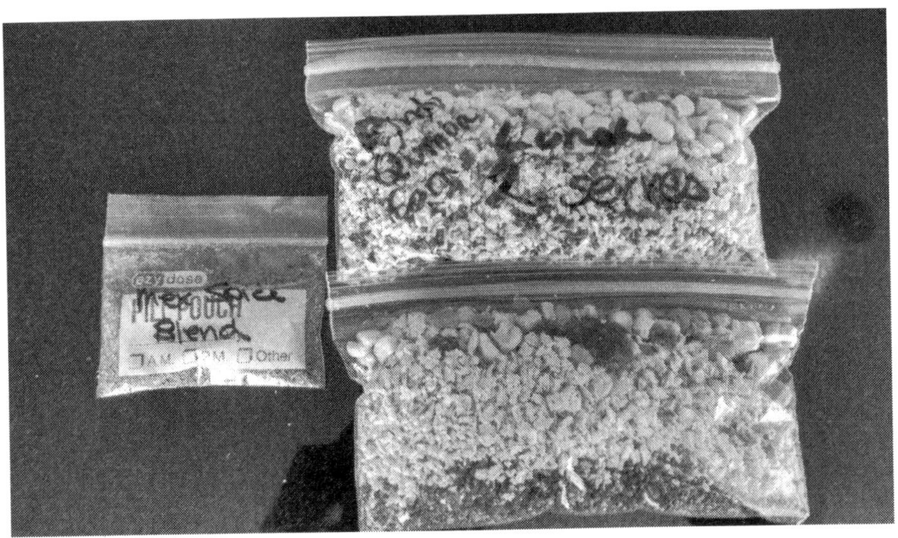

Lunch packets with dehydrated beans, freeze-dried veggies and Mexican spices

Week 4: Dinner Focus

- Monday: Assess your supplies and purchase needed dinner items. If you're creating recipes from dry ingredients, make sure you have all the spices and ingredients from each recipe you're using. Allow a couple of hours to get your shopping list together.
- Tuesday: Go to the store and get needed items.
- Saturday: Create an assembly line and package dinner items. If you're using the recipes from Chapter 11 this may take two full days or more for a month-long trip. You will likely eat the same meal a few times during the trip so check your menu and line up bags for one recipe at a time, with perhaps three-to-five repetitions of the same meal. If there are variations in the ingredients you want to use, fill each bag with the basic ingredients and then top off with the variations.

Week 4 sample shopping list:

- Freeze-dried meal packets
- Ingredients for meals you're assembling (varies considerably but staples might include ramen packets, instant mashed potatoes, freeze-dried rice, dehydrated bean flakes, freeze-dried vegetables, freeze-dried meats, nuts, freeze-dried cheese and spices).

Week 5: Snacks, Drinks and Zero Day Focus

- Monday: Assess your supplies and purchase needed items. If you're planning to take zero days (rest days with no hiking, i.e. zero mileage) at your resupply locations, plan the food and other luxuries you might want to pack for those days and take into consideration whether that location has food for purchase. Allow a couple of hours to get your shopping list together.
- Tuesday: Go to the store and get needed items.
- Saturday: Create an assembly line and distribute snacks for each day. Package drink powders in the container of your choice. Create a group of foods for your resupply treats. Allow a full day for this task for a month-long trip.

Week 5 sample shopping list

- Hydration/electrolyte powder
- Energy bars (regular and high-protein)
- Energy gels or gummies
- Powdered whole milk (if not already purchased on Week 1)
- Coffee or tea (if not already purchased on Week 1)
- Water flavorings (e.g. Crystal Light, Tang, True Lemon, etc.)
- Zero day treats (see Chapter 14)

One box for each leg of the journey

Week 6: Final Count and Packaging by Trip Section

After all the work assembling and packaging food, it might seem like this part would be fast. In some ways, it is. However, it may take longer than you think. One person reported that they spent an entire day just seeing if they could fit everything into their bear barrel for the longest section. Allow a full day to do this work for a month-long trip, longer for a multi-month trip.

- Friday: Purchase fresh foods the day before mailing.

- Saturday:
    - See the "Count and Recount" section below in this chapter.
    - Designate a physical space for each day in a section (e.g. Day 1-5). If you're taking a zero day, allocate a separate space for those items.
    - Place each day's breakfast, lunch, dinner, snacks and drinks together. When you are satisfied that you have everything, put

them all together in the box or bucket that you plan to use for mailing (be sure you know which type of container is accepted by your resupply location by checking their website). Place a prominent note on the box if last minute items, such as tortillas or cheese, need to be added before sealing.

- If desired, like items can be packaged together. Options include rubber-banding all the breakfast baggies together and storing lunches and dinners in gallon-zip top bag. Liquids or cheeses should be double bagged in freezer-bags in case of leakage. It is easier to fit food in bear canisters if they are not bagged together. The gallon bags can be used as garbage bags or storage bags for other items.
- Include extra zip-top bags of all sizes in the resupply.

Week 6 sample shopping list

- Tortillas
- String cheese or other cheeses
- Salami or other cured meats

Jessica's meals are organized into plastic bags with color-coded labels: blue for breakfast, yellow for lunch, green for dinner (Photo by Jessica Scott)

Summary

- Have a plan. See six-week sample plan.
- Make a menu.
- Gather any needed supplies, including food, containers and mailing supplies.
- Keep hands and food clean to reduce microbial contamination.
- Dedicate space to store your food during the planning process.
- Count and recount your meals.

Chapter 5: Breakfast

Breakfast is pretty easy, so get this one out of the way first. Assemble your preferred breakfast foods and large quantities of snack size baggies. Then start measuring and zipping the bags shut. Before you know it you'll have a multitude of breakfast meals ready to go. Coffee and tea are addressed in Chapter 9 with other drinks, but you can assemble your morning drinks here if you wish.

Cereal

Cold or hot cereal is the easiest to manage in the morning, when most hikers are anxious to break down camp and get back on the trail. Granola or other cold cereals are fast and easy. Instant oatmeal takes just a little more time and can be warm and satisfying on a cold morning. Other hot cereal ideas include cream of wheat, cream of rice, multi-grain cereals, grits and quinoa. A variety of toppings can enhance hot or cold cereal, including sweet or savory additions. Sometimes the sweet breakfasts get monotonous and a savory breakfast, perhaps with grits or quinoa, is welcome. All you need to do for most cereal is add milk, and breakfast is done.

Since we've already established that my husband can eat the same thing every single day without burning out, he gets instant oatmeal, two packages per day. I, on the other hand, am not particularly fond of breakfast. I like granola and oatmeal is OK for a few mornings. I might plan for 2-3 days of granola, then one day of oatmeal. I don't care for the gluey texture of some instant oatmeal so I experimented with different brands and found that the Trader Joe's instant oatmeal was more to my liking.

After repackaging the granola or oatmeal into snack-size baggies I add different freeze-dried fruits for variety. One bag gets blueberries, another gets raspberries, the third day gets strawberries and I might go wild and have one day with all kinds of mixed berries. I also ratchet up the texture and protein component with chopped hazelnuts, flax seeds and chia seeds. I add powdered full fat milk to the oatmeal baggies at home to add calories and protein. In camp, I also mix up a cup of reconstituted milk, in addition to the amount that was added to the baggie, for my granola and tea.

Some people, especially those who rise early, prefer a quick snack of nuts and fruit or an energy bar while they break down camp. They like to start hiking immediately to warm up in the chilly morning air. Then they find a pleasing spot to have a "second breakfast" when the sun is up.

Hot cereal

- Instant oatmeal
- Cream of wheat
- Cream of rice
- Instant multi-grain cereal
- Instant grits
- Instant quinoa flakes
- Quinoa (whole grain, cooked and dehydrated)

Cold cereal:

- Granola
- Muesli
- Packaged breakfast cereals

Assorted breakfast cereals and toppings

Cereal Toppings

There are endless sweet or savory toppings to consider adding to hot or cold cereal. Here are a few.

- Freeze-dried blueberries
- Freeze-dried raspberries
- Freeze-dried strawberries
- Chopped dried dates
- Raisins
- Dried cranberry
- Banana chips
- Dried apples
- Dried apricots
- Flax seeds
- Chia seeds
- Hemp hearts (seeds)

- Chopped hazelnuts
- Slivered almonds
- Chopped walnuts
- Chopped pecans
- Chopped peanuts
- Chopped cashews
- Macadamia nut pieces
- Brazil nut pieces
- Shredded coconut
- Chocolate chips
- Cacao nibs
- Cocoa powder
- Oat bran
- Wheat bran
- Brown sugar
- Maple sugar
- Honey crystals
- Cinnamon
- Full-fat powdered milk
- Powdered almond milk
- Powdered soy milk
- Powdered coconut milk
- Bran

For hot cereal, in addition to the above:

- Ghee
- Olive oil
- Coconut oil
- Powdered butter
- Freeze-dried vegetables
- Dried meats

- Aged fresh or freeze-dried cheese
- Protein powder
- Powdered peanut butter

Milk

Full fat powdered milk is a vast improvement in flavor compared to the non-fat milk you find in grocery stores. Unfortunately it can be hard to find, though ethnic stores may carry it. Thankfully, Peak, Nido and other brands are available from on-line retailers.

Eggs and More

If you prefer a hot non-cereal breakfast, there are commercial freeze-dried options, including scrambled eggs with or without bacon, eggs with hash browns and sausage, biscuits and gravy and more. You can supplement these meals with extra freeze-dried sausage from a bulk can to increase calories if you have a hearty appetite at breakfast. I don't mind the Styrofoam texture of powdered eggs when they are mixed with other foods, especially if smothered with a packet of ketchup and hot sauce. It reminds me of those halcyon days in my college dorm when I'd nurse a hangover with powdered eggs and Diet Coke.

OvaEasy egg crystals can be scrambled or made into an omelet, either in a pot or freezer-bag. Mix the egg product with water in a baggie, drop in some freeze dried veggies, cheese, herbs or shelf-stable bacon. Immerse the bag in hot (not actively boiling) water for five to ten minutes until solidified. I have not had success reconstituting OvaEasy eggs by simply adding hot water to the crystals, as you can do with other freezer-bag meals.

Many hikers don't like to spend the time preparing breakfast but breakfast foods can be a viablemeal at any time of day. An egg scramble in the evening can be an appealing dinner choice.

Fourteen Unique Breakfasts

FOURTEEN UNIQUE BREAKFASTS			
Day	**Ingredient #1**	**Ingredient #2**	**Ingredient #3**
1	Oatmeal	Dried blueberries	Chopped walnuts
2	Granola	Dried strawberries	Chia seeds
3	Grits	Raisins	Brown sugar
4	Muesli	Dried raspberries	Flax seeds
5	Cream of wheat	Shredded coconut	Macadamia nut pieces
6	Quinoa	Cocoa	Slivered almonds
7	Eggs	Dried salsa	Freeze-dried sausage
8	Oatmeal	Powdered peanut butter	Hemp hearts
9	Granola	Dried cranberry	Chia seeds
10	Grits	Chopped hazelnuts	Brown sugar
11	Muesli	Dried dates	Flax seeds
12	Cream of rye	Chocolate chips	Chopped almonds
13	Quinoa flakes	Cinnamon powder	Chopped pecans
14	Eggs	Ketchup packet	Freeze-dried cheese

Summary

- Cold or hot cereal is the easiest option.
- Cereal toppings can add a great deal of variety and can enhance calorie and protein counts.
- Eggs and savory dishes are available.

Chapter 6: Lunch

Lunches seem to be hardest for many people to come up with, including me. If people post questions on the internet hiking group about meal choices, it's often people begging for lunch ideas. Most don't want to set up a stove, so quick, easily prepared lunches are desirable. Calories have already been burned with the morning's hike and generally several more hours loom ahead by the time it's midday. Replenishing lost calories and electrolytes is important at this time, though some like to snack throughout the day. For those who desire a longer rest break, a tasty lunch is something to look forward to.

Tortilla-Based Lunch

Like others, I have experienced challenges planning lunch. I have finally come up with a strategy that works for us. My current lunch plan is based on the venerable tortilla. I resisted tortillas for a long time because they are heavy. However, I found that their weight is compensated by their extreme versatility, palatability and ease of packing. To store them in the bear canister, I stand the package of tortillas up against the side of the can and pack other foods around them. A standard brand (Mission or La Tortilla Factory, for example) will not go bad for a looooong, long time without refrigeration (at least a month), especially if left in an unopened package. If you do repackage them, avoid touching the tortillas with your hands to prevent contamination. Do not use preservative-free, specialty, organic tortillas as they will go bad quickly. Take a look at this test performed by Packit Gourmet (bit.ly/2o5wbTP).

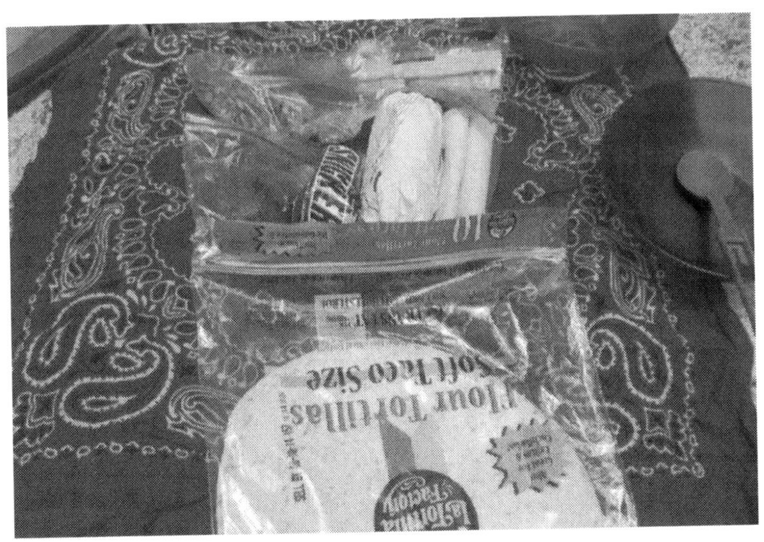

Tortillas can be stuffed with an endless variety of foods

A variety of foods can go into the tortilla. For me, this includes dehydrated bean mixes that I purchase or make myself. Natural food stores often carry a black bean mix in the bulk bins. I make my own by cooking up a big batch of black, pinto, white or other beans, mashing them on a flat surface and dehydrating them. I add spices later. I also cook different types of Indian lentils and dehydrate. The small, flat lentils are a consistency that doesn't require mashing. Mixed with spices and other toppings, you can create a tasty lunch relatively quickly.

I also cook and then dehydrate batches of grains such as brown rice, white rice and quinoa. An option that takes less time is to get freeze-dried rice, which rehydrates even better than home dehydrated rice. Couscous is another choice and doesn't have to be cooked ahead of time. I usually combine the grains with the bean mixture, but they can stand alone.

I love fresh salsa so I dehydrate my favorite kind, full of chunks of tomatoes and hot peppers, into leather (like a fruit roll, only made with salsa). I also do Sriracha sauce leather. I've had these grow mold after several months in the past so now I'm careful to wear gloves when handling the leather and package it separately. I tear it or break it into small pieces that can be added to meals.

When I'm ready to portion out our lunches, I fill a third of a snack baggie with beans or lentils, a third with a grain, and then I add spices and extras. The beans usually get a Mexican or Cajun spice mix, the lentils a Moroccan or Indian spice mix and I might throw some chia seeds in for good measure. If I'm going to consume the lunch within a week or two, I'll add a piece of salsa leather; otherwise I'll have small "pill-pouch" baggies with salsa that can be added on the trail.

Another good mix from the natural food store is a tabbouleh mix, to which I add raisins, dried cranberry or freeze-dried grapes.

There are many variations on tortilla stuffing, including peanut or other nut butter, honey, jam, Nutella, tuna packets, hummus, and anything else you can think of.

Other Lunch Ideas

Instead of tortillas, consider using crackers, pita chips, bagels and other "topping holders." Crackers with sliced salami and cheese are a trail favorite.

Cheese and cured meats are ancient methods of preserving food. The only caveat is that some modern cured and aged foods are not aged as long as they once were, or methods might have changed and they may have a relatively short life-span. Be sure to read labels for cured meats and note whether they state that refrigeration is required.

Hard cheeses such as cheddar, processed cheeses (American), and both block and grated Parmesan do not require refrigeration. I have found that individually wrapped string cheese sticks last a long time. The small round individually wrapped soft cheeses that are encased in wax (e.g. Baby Bell) last a long time, too. By "long time," I mean several weeks. Cured meats (e.g. dry aged salami) can last for many days, especially if care is taken to not handle them ahead of time with bare hands. Hard/dry sausages, such as Genoa salami, sopressata and pepperoni, are shelf-stable for 6 weeks if whole. After the casing is cut into, meats should be used within a few days. Try to find small cured meats rather than one large log.

It's possible to make a decent tuna salad or chicken salad on the trail if you bring packets of condiments. Pasta salads are another idea that some hikers use, though I tend to gravitate toward these kinds of recipes for dinner.

If you have the time or inclination to pull out the stove to heat some water on the trail, another good choice is soup. The natural food stores usually have several types of instant soup mixes that can be warm and filling. Ramen is another choice, though the flavor packets usually contain MSG. See the "Asian Ramen Blend" and "Simple Healthy Ramen" recipes for healthy ramen options. Some foods to add to ramen or soup are freeze-dried vegetables, bits of jerky, powdered egg and nuts. Ramen has the added benefit of not requiring hot water. If you add cold water to ramen in a bag at breakfast, it'll be softened by lunch.

Early in my backpacking career I had trouble figuring out why I bonked in the afternoon. I'd get downright disoriented, wandering off the trail and not making any sense. We solved the problem by stopping for a real lunch, boiling water in a pot and making ramen. It may have been the rest break, the electrolytes or maybe more calories than our snack lunch alternative at the time. For years we maintained this routine and it worked. Then I burned out and the thought of ramen in any form started making me gag. That's when we switched to tortilla-based lunches. I'm just starting to come back around to ramen, especially the healthier ramen options that are available now.

On the Trail

In the morning, while I'm eating breakfast, I gather our lunch supplies and put them in a separate ditty bag. It goes in an outside pouch in my pack so we don't have to get the bear canister out during the day. I reconstitute the bean mix or tabbouleh in two plastic Ball Freezer Jars. A baggie can work, but can be messy. These jars, though somewhat bulky, only weigh one ounce, including the top. I add half of the baggie's contents into each jar, one for me and one for Steve, add warm or cold water (it doesn't matter which) and place the jars in a gallon-size zip top bag in case of leakage. I may add a piece of dehydrated salsa or Sriracha sauce to add some zip.

Extra food goes into the lunch bag. This includes Tanka Bites (buffalo-cranberry bar) for me, salami for Steve, string cheese or individual wax-coated cheese for each of us and a baggie of seeds. The seed bag contains a mixture of pumpkin seeds, sunflower seeds and freeze-dried corn, which gives the tortilla mixture a satisfying crunch.

At lunchtime, I lay out a clean bandana that I keep in our lunch bag. I place a tortilla on top and load it up. Steve eats his salami and cheese separately while I pile everything in the tortilla: first the beans and rice (which by lunchtime is soft and pliable), then a layer of seeds and corn, and then long, thin strips of string cheese that I tear apart. At the end, I gently press three or four Tanka bites down the center and roll it up.

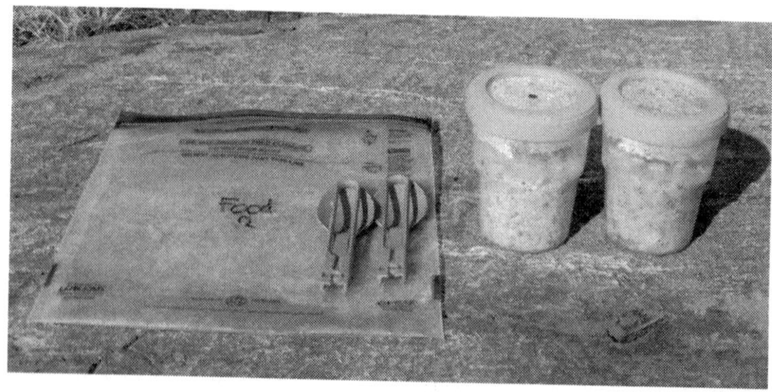

Lunch is rehydrating in plastic jars

Ultra-Light Lunches

Ultra-light (UL) lunches rely on mostly dehydrated or freeze-dried food.

Grain or legume base:

- Black bean flakes (dehydrated)
- Pinto bean flakes (dehydrated)
- Red bean flakes (dehydrated)
- Lentils (dehydrated)
- Rice-white or brown (dehydrated)
- Quinoa (dehydrated)
- Tabbouleh
- Hummus (dehydrated)

Toppings:

- Spices (see Chapter 10-Spice Blends)
- Freeze-dried corn or other vegetables
- Freeze-dried fruit
- Nuts (cashew, almond, hazelnut pieces, etc.)
- Seeds (pumpkin, sunflower, flax, chia, etc.)
- Dried meats (bacon bits, Tanka Bites, jerky bits, salami, etc.)
- Cheese (string cheese, aged, hard cheeses, etc.)
- Dehydrated salsa or hot sauce
- Pesto powder

Wrap

- Tortillas (not so light, but a good wrap)
- Pita

Tortilla with beans, rice, corn, pumpkin seeds, salsa and Tanka Bites

Light Lunches

Add some heavier foods that add significant taste and texture. You can either choose to carry the extra weight for each day, bring just a few for a treat or just use them during shorter training hikes. See the UL section above for the basic strategy for assembling lunches.

- Tuna packets
- Chicken packets
- Dried fruit
- Packets of condiments such as mayonnaise, mustard
- Peanut butter packets
- Ramen
- Instant soups such as corn chowder or bean flakes

Heavy Lunches

I wouldn't bring these on a long-distance unless it was a resupply stop because they are too heavy. For a shorter training hike it's a luxury to have fresh or canned foods. On our week-long canoeing trips on the Yukon River we bring some of these foods. See the UL section for the basic strategy for assembling lunches.

- Cans of chicken or tuna salad
- Potted meats
- Sardines
- Firm avocado
- Fresh fruit such as apples
- Bagel

Fresh food is a real treat the first day on the trail

Fourteen Unique Lunches

FOURTEEN UNIQUE LUNCHES						
Day	**Ingredient #1**	**Ingredient #2**	**Ingredient #3**	**Ingredient #4**	**Ingredient #5**	**Ingredient #6**
1	Tortilla	Dehydrated black beans	Freeze-dried brown rice	Freeze-dried corn	Flax & chia seeds	Mexican Spice Blend
2	Crackers	Dehydrated hummus	Mixed vegetables	Sesame seeds	Lemon oil	Moroccan Spice Blend
3	Tortilla	Peanut butter	Jam packet			
4	Crackers	Sausage or salami	String cheese			
5	Tortilla	Tuna in foil packet	Mayonnaise packet	Mustard packet	Relish packet	
6	Ramen	Freeze-dried mixed vegetables	Dried mushrooms	Sesame seeds	Sesame oil	Ramen Spice Blend
7	Tortilla	Dehydrated pinto beans	Freeze-dried white rice	Freeze-dried mixed vegetables	Pumpkin seeds	Dehydrated salsa
8	Tortilla	Tabbuleh	Freeze-dried grapes	Sun-dried tomato	Chopped nuts	Lemon oil
9	Tortilla	Salmon in foil packet	Mayonnaise packet	Relish packet		
10	Tortilla	Dehydrated lentils	Freeze-dried white rice	Freeze-dried broccoli	Hemp seeds	Indian Spice Blend
11	Crackers	Dehydrated hummus	Sundried tomatoes	Pumpkin seeds	Pesto or salsa	
12	Tortilla	Dehydrated red beans	Dehydrated farro or bulgur	Freeze-dried grean beans	Sunflower seeds	Cajun Spice Blend
13	Tortilla	Peanut butter	Honey	Banana chips		
14	Rice Ramen	Salmon in foil packet	Freeze-dried mixed vegetables	Dried mushrooms	Sesame oil	Ramen Spice Blend

Summary

- Tortillas last a long time without going bad and are a convenient receptacle for many different food items.
- Crackers or bread can substitute for tortillas.
- Other lunch ideas include soup and ramen.

Chapter 7: Dinner

Dinners take some thought. Most people look forward to dinner as a time when the hard work of the day is done. Hopefully you've found a nice campsite with a good view and you're able to relax near a lake or stream. Whereas breakfast and lunch are often hurried affairs when you're anxious to make your miles and see what's around the next corner, evening is a time when you can look forward to a hot, tasty meal. Your body needs calories to stay warm through the night and your muscles are crying out for replenishing protein and nutrients. The time you put into planning good evening meals will reward you on the trail with a warm feeling in your tummy when you go to bed.

This is really where the three strategies outlined in Chapter 1 kick in. You have to decide if you're going to buy packaged foods such as Mountain House, Backpacker's Pantry, Backpacker Gourmet or other brands (easiest), dehydrate all of your own meals (most time consuming) or something in between.

If you decide to make your own, you don't need a different meal for every night. To make it more efficient, pick a few different recipes and make several dinners. You could vary some ingredients to change it up. For example, you could make a Thai food dinner with rice for one meal and noodles for another. You could make barbecued chicken with mashed sweet potato for one meal and instant mashed potatoes for another. Substitute beef and couscous for Moroccan tabbouleh with lamb for a different flavor profile. See Chapter 11 for dinner recipes to assemble from dry ingredients and Chapter 12 for inspiration for meals to make at home and dehydrate.

Grits with mushrooms, sausage and peas

Trail Staples

Olive oil is a standby in our mess kit. A big dollop of olive oil added to our dinner while it rehydrates improves the flavor and adds valuable fat and calories. I use a range of one teaspoon to one tablespoon per person. Some prefer other oils such as ghee (has the benefit of being a solid at room temperature), coconut oil (also a solid at room temperature), walnut oil and others. I sometimes bring some lemon oil or sesame oil but find that, for a thru-hike, simple is better. Oil without a distinctive flavor is more versatile. Keep in mind that the oils that are in solid form at room temperature will not be able to dissolve in cold water if you plan to do any rehydrating with cold water. The melting point of ghee is 96 degrees Fahrenheit; for coconut oil, it's 78 degrees Fahrenheit. I package olive oil in a Nalgene bottle and bag it in a freezer baggie, though I've never had it leak. I would not use a brand other than Nalgene unless it was thoroughly tested.

I add spices to my individual trail meals and I also carry a small spice kit. Currently I only carry salt, pepper and red pepper flakes, while in the past I have also carried an herb blend or other spice blends.

Trail Testing

No matter which way you decide to go, try to take some shakedown trips to make sure you like the foods you select, unless you have a lot of backcountry experience and already know this. At home, I love exotic, spicy flavors—the hotter the better. Indian, Moroccan, Mexican, Thai, Indonesian—it's all good. I learned that on the trail, my stomach sometimes does back flips and the thought of curry is enough to make me gag. I tried hemp hearts and thought they had a neutral flavor. On the trail I found that they actually had a subtle flavor I didn't care for in my oatmeal, whereas I love the nutty flavor of roasted flax seeds. We've learned to play it safe with choices that are flavorful but a little blander than what we're used to. It's easier to add hot pepper flakes, dehydrated salsa or some spices on the trail than to not be able to face dinner at night. I never eat creamy pasta dishes at home, but they taste pretty good while on the trail. On the other hand, a friend who normally likes mild food craves some heat when she's on the trail. You'll never know what works for you until you get out there and see. If you don't have time to do that before your thru-hike, bring a wide variety of foods. You don't want to have 28 days of Mexican foods with you and find that you crave fettuccini.

Extras

If you have the space, bring some extra tortillas, cheese and maybe some jerky or salami for an appetizer. I sometimes get really hungry about a half an hour after we quit hiking. Knowing that it will be awhile before dinner is ready, I'll have a snack or drink to tide me over. If I haven't eaten my entire 20-gram protein bar, I'll finish it off then, otherwise I know I'll have to eat it after dinner. I found it easier to pack some extra goodies for the stretches on the first half but had to reduce them for the longest stretch as there simply wasn't room in our bear canisters.

A stack of chocolate bars is all that is needed for dessert

Dessert

Think about some something you would like to satisfy your sweet tooth. Our standby is chocolate (white, milk or dark chocolate). It's a nice end-of-the-day treat and provides some extra fat calories to help stay warm. Some people like to make freeze-dried desserts or carry some cookies. See Chapter 13 for "A Simple Special Occasion Dessert" for birthdays, anniversaries or an emergency treat to salvage a tough day.

Fourteen Unique Dinners

FOURTEEN UNIQUE DINNERS	
Day	**Dinner Recipes**
1	Simple Healthy Ramen
2	BBQ Chicken with Mashed Potatoes
3	Moroccan Tabbouleh with Beef
4	Italian Sausage and Orzo Pasta
5	Mexican Black Bean and Quinoa Wrap
6	Chinese Cashew Chicken Noodles
7	Cajun Chicken, Sausage and Rice
8	Indonesian Chicken Noodles
9	Beef Stew with Mashed Sweet Potato
10	Thai Curry Chicken and Rice
11	Hearty Grits with Sausage and Veggies
12	Indian Chicken, Lentils and Quinoa
13	Italian Chicken and Farro
14	Moroccan Couscous with Lamb

Summary

- Decide on your approach to dinners: buy packaged freeze-dried meals (easiest), dehydrate all of your own meals (most time consuming) or something in between.
- Put together a small kit of trail staples, such as olive oil, salt and pepper, to add to meals.
- Test foods on short backpacking trips before a long thru-hike to make sure they are palatable to you.
- If you have any additional room, pack some extras of your favorite foods.
- Think about something sweet, even if you don't normally eat candy or desserts.

- See Chapter 11 for dinner recipes to assemble from dry ingredients and Chapter 12 for inspiration for meals to make at home and dehydrate.

Chapter 8: Snacks

Some people don't prepare lunches at all. They just bring enough snacks to carry them through the day. We like regular meals, including lunch, and bring snacks to supplement calories during the day and at camp.

Many snack foods can be purchased in bulk from bulk bins at supermarkets. Granola or protein bars can be purchased and there are many recipes online for homemade bars.

Bring a variety of flavors

Snack Ideas

- Nuts (almonds, cashews, walnuts, pecans, macadamia, Brazil nuts, peanuts, pistachios, mixed nuts, etc.)
- Seeds (pumpkin, sunflower, etc.)
- Jerky (beef, turkey, venison, salmon, etc.)
- Salami
- Sausage (dry aged)
- Tanka bars and bites (buffalo and cranberry)
- Candy (lemon drops, gourmet jelly beans, licorice, pastilles, Skittles, M&Ms, peanut M&Ms, etc.)
- Candy bars (Snickers, PayDay, KitKat, etc.)
- Energy bars (Clif, Kind, ProBar, Stinger, Tanka, GoMacro, Bobo's Oat Bars, etc.)
- Energy gels
- Honey sesame bars
- Cheese (aged cheeses, string cheese, individual cheese encased in wax, etc.)
- Dried fruit (mango, apricot, dates, apple, mandarin orange, persimmon, etc.)
- Fruit leather
- Plantain chips
- Carob chips
- GORP (Good Ol' Raisins and Peanuts—or anything you want to add)

Summary

- Bring a variety of snacks to supplement calories.
- Purchase snacks or make your own.

Chapter 9: Drinks

Water is an excellent choice for hydration, but sometimes it's not enough. Electrolytes are also essential (see Chapter 3). Electrolytes can be obtained through food or electrolyte drink powder. Sometimes water tastes different on the trail, so some prefer using drink powders to flavor their beverage.

We don't generally drink a lot of alcohol on the trail because we're too tired or it's just not appealing. We each bring a small bottle for those nights when a cocktail at sunset is just the ticket. Or, there are those days when everything went wrong and you just want a shot of alcohol and to go to bed. Vodka and orange Tang or lemonade is quite refreshing, while brandy and hot chocolate is a great way to chase away the chill of a Sierra evening.

Water Purification

Unless you're a big risk-taker, water should be purified in most backcountry areas. Choices include mechanical filtration (e.g. Sawyer Squeeze gravity filter, Katadyn pump filter), UV light (e.g SteriPen), chemical tablets or drops (e.g. AquaMira chlorine tablets), boiling water (effective if water is brought to a full rolling boil for one to five minutes). There are pros and cons to each method. Gravity filters can take more time than other methods, and must be back flushed regularly. They can be difficult to fill in shallow water. Pump filters take some effort to operate and the filters can clog over time, especially with heavy silt or glacial flour. The SteriPen uses batteries so extra sets of batteries must be carried. Anything mechanical or electronic can break. Some chemical tablets or drops can leave a taste. Drops can accidentally leak out of a bottle and tablets could get moist and disintegrate if the cap isn't on tight. Boiling water is fuel-intensive.

We use a SteriPen in the Sierra, where the water runs crystal clear and is well-known for its pure taste. We also use a SteriPen when traveling overseas. When we are in the backcountry in a place where the water might be silty, such as the Yukon where glacial dust creates cloudy water, we use a Katadyn mechanical filter. When I'm solo and just want something lightweight and easy, I occasionally use chlorine tablets. We try not to go overboard with backup systems, though we generally have a few emergency options. For the SteriPen, we carry extra batteries, including a set with the emergency supplies, over and above whatever we think is enough. I keep a few chlorine tablets in my emergency kit. I carry a small bottle of bleach to use for laundry and we've used that to purify water in a pinch. We usually boil our cooking water, so it's not always necessary to purify it using other means.

A SteriPen is one way to purify water

Storing Drink Powders

Drink powders can be stored in zip-top baggies (double-bagged), lightweight plastic jars or collapsible bottles. I started using flexible bottles designed to be used as a water bottle because I liked the idea of having more space as the supply was used, being able to pour from a spout, having a secure cap, and having a sturdy receptacle that wasn't likely to get punctured. I use 250- or 500-ml collapsible bottles. Using a funnel, I pour the powders from their original container into the bottle. To use the powder I unscrew the cap, pour the powder into my cup and add water to the cup. Water never gets added to the container with the powder.

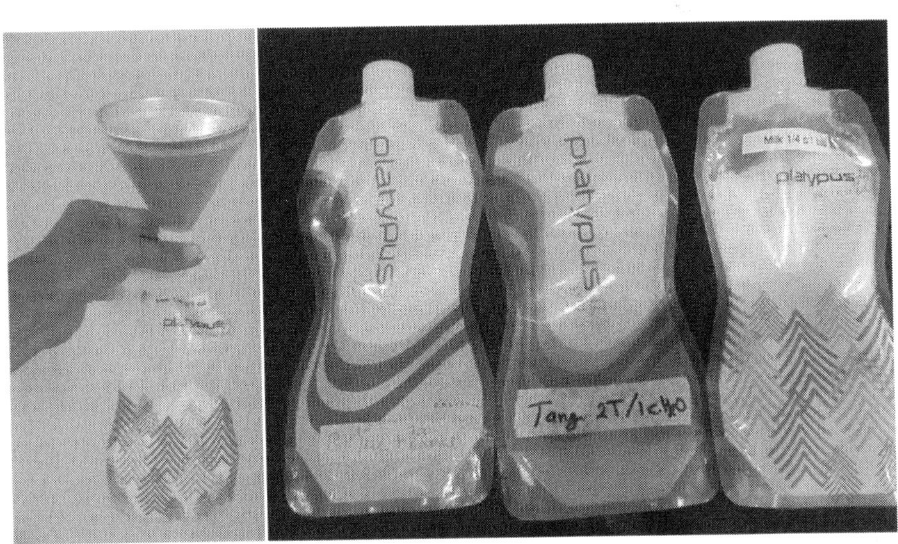

Pour the drink powder into a flexible container with a funnel (shown here with Platypus SoftBottle)

Drink Choices

- Instant coffee (e.g. Starbucks Via individual packets)
- Tea (with and without caffeine, black, green, fruit-flavored)
- Hot chocolate instant mix (add extra milk for more calories)
- Strawberry milk powder
- Powdered milk (full fat whole milk, e.g. Peak or Nido)
- Hydration mix with electrolytes (Skratch Labs, Gu, Nuun, etc.)
- Tang or KoolAid mixes (mostly sugar, not exactly healthy but are aspartame-free)
- True Citrus flavors such as lemon, lime, orange, grapefruit and more
- Crystal Light (contains aspartame)
- Alcohol (vodka, tequila, brandy, whiskey, etc.)

Summary

- Decide on the method of water purification you want to use.
- Bring a variety of drinks to add flavor and calories.

Chapter 10: Spice Blends

Creating your own spice blends allows you to know exactly what is in them. You can make up batches in the dark days of winter and have them ready to go when you assemble your backpacking meals in spring or summer.

I can't eat a lot of commercially prepared spice blends because I can't be certain what is in them. I don’t have anything against MSG per se, but they can be a migraine trigger and that has become a problem for me in recent years. Many ingredients in commercial blends are similar to MSG (more than 40 ingredients contain MSG or MSG-like substances) and some additives don't even need to be listed on food labels. Most ramen spice packets are full of MSG and they don't even try to disguise it with other names.

The spice blend recipes do not contain salt. If you are going to use the spice blends in the recipes that follow, know that the recipes contain salt. If you are going to use the spice blends in your own recipes, you can add ½ teaspoon salt or to taste if you wish. Keep in mind that it’s easier to add salt than subtract it.

All of the spices and herbs in the recipes are dried, not fresh.

Asian Ramen Blend

The first spice blend I developed was for ramen noodles when we discovered that a close friend and backpacking partner didn't tolerate MSG. It doesn't taste exactly like the spice packet but it's tasty.

1 teaspoon ginger
1 teaspoon garlic powder
1 teaspoon pepper
½ teaspoon Five Spice powder
½ teaspoon cumin
⅛-¼ teaspoon red pepper flakes (optional)

About 4 servings

Notes: See Simple Healthy Ramen recipe, which includes Umami Dust powder and mushroom powder. Flavor variations can be created by using curry or powdered coconut cream instead of Five Spice powder. Chicken or vegetable bouillon can be added (be aware that many bouillon products contain MSG or related substances).

Indian Spice Blend

Use caution with curry blends as they can taste very strong. I love curry at home but find I can't tolerate it on the trail. I'm including it for those who have an adventurous palate and want to try it. It's best to toast the dry spices to mellow the flavors.

½ teaspoon turmeric
½ teaspoon ground ginger
½ teaspoon cumin
½ teaspoon garlic powder
¼ teaspoon ground cardamom
¼ teaspoon black pepper
¼ teaspoon red pepper flakes (optional)
⅛ teaspoon cinnamon
⅛ teaspoon ground cloves

About 3 servings

Optional: Toast the spices by placing the spice mix in a dry skillet with med-high flame. Heat for 1-2 minutes until it becomes aromatic and the color darkens slightly.

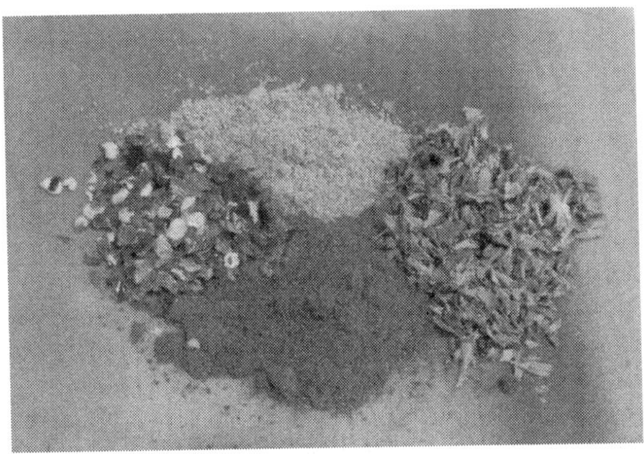

Indian Spice Blend with curry, paprika, oregano and crushed red pepper

Mexican Spice Blend

If you use a blend of different dried chilis (available at Mexican food stores or online retailers) you'll get a complex flavor profile that enhances rice and beans considerably. Do not use chili powder that already contains other spices.

1½ teaspoon pure ground chili
1 teaspoon paprika
½ teaspoon oregano
½ teaspoon onion powder
¼ teaspoon cumin
¼ teaspoon garlic powder
¼ teaspoon black pepper
Pinch chipotle powder (optional)
Pinch red pepper flakes or cayenne powder (optional)

About 4 servings

Italian Spice Blend

1 teaspoon dried basil
1 teaspoon dried oregano
1 teaspoon dried thyme
1 teaspoon dried marjoram
1 teaspoon dried parsley
¼ teaspoon garlic powder
¼ teaspoon black pepper
Pinch red pepper flakes (optional)

About 5 servings

Note: Italian spice blends can be found pre-mixed in many supermarkets if you don't want to create your own.

Thai Spice Blend

2 teaspoons paprika
1 teaspoon ground coriander
½ teaspoon ground cumin
½ teaspoon ground ginger
½ teaspoon dry mustard
½ teaspoon dried basil
½ teaspoon curry
¼ teaspoon cayenne powder or red pepper flakes (optional)
¼ teaspoon garlic powder
¼ teaspoon black pepper

About 3-7 servings (1 teaspoon vs 2 teaspoons)

Reviewer Notes:
One reviewer gave this a top score and said it was a “very good spice blend”. Another reviewer prefers just a hint of ginger so she reduced the ginger to ¼ teaspoon and added 2 teaspoon of curry powder (I added a small amount of curry to the spice blend above).

Another reviewer used ⅛ teaspoon of cayenne AND red pepper flakes as she likes spicy food. She didn’t add any salt.

Moroccan Spice Blend

1 teaspoon ground ginger
½ teaspoon cinnamon
½ teaspoon garlic powder
¼ teaspoon cumin
¼ teaspoon cloves
¼ teaspoon nutmeg
¼ teaspoon ground cloves
¼ teaspoon black pepper

About 3 servings

Cajun Spice Blend

2 teaspoon smoked paprika (or regular)
1 teaspoon oregano
1 teaspoon thyme
1 teaspoon basil
1 teaspoon garlic powder
½ teaspoon onion powder
¼ teaspoon cumin
¼ teaspoon ground chilis, such as ancho peppers (optional)
¼ teaspoon red pepper flakes (optional)
¼ teaspoon black pepper
Pinch of allspice

About 7 servings

Mushroom Gravy

1 tablespoon chopped dried mushrooms
1 teaspoon dried porcini mushroom powder (or porcini or morel powder)
½ teaspoon onion powder
¼ teaspoon powdered milk
⅛ teaspoon thyme
⅛ teaspoon black pepper
Pinch of salt (optional)

Mix all ingredients with 1-2 tablespoons hot water on the trail.

1 serving

Notes: Vegetable powder can add richness to the gravy. Try celery, carrot, tomato or others. Purchase or make your own from ground dehydrated vegetables. If you don't have an issue with "natural flavorings," which may or may not contain MSG, try ¼ teaspoon Umami Dust Powder.

Homemade Poultry Bouillon

Bouillon has been omitted from recipes because the commercial products contain MSG or MSG-like substances that some people are sensitive to. Homemade bouillon can enhance gravies, soups and many of the recipes in the next chapter. The terminology can overlap but stock or bone broth is made with bones and meat (and may include vegetables), broth is technically just made with meat and bouillon refers to dehydrated stock.

1 turkey carcass or 3-4 chicken carcasses
2 diced carrots (optional)
1 diced celery stick (optional)
1 diced onion (optional)
1 clove of garlic (optional)
salt (optional but not recommended due to the concentrated form of the final product)

Instructions

- Add 4 quarts of water to the carcass with the vegetables.
- Bring to a boil and then slowly simmer for 2-6 (up to 24) hours, skimming off any foam.
- Strain the broth and discard vegetables.
- Refrigerate broth overnight and then skim the fat off the top.
- Boil until reduced to thick syrup.
- Pour onto dehydrator trays with liners (fruit roll liners) and dehydrate at 135 degrees. This can take 24 (for leather) to 48 hours (brittle). When completely dry and brittle, grind to make bouillon powder. One tsp. of powder will reconstitute to one cup of broth.

Yield: about 5 oz.

Variation: Homemade stock can be made with chicken, beef or other meat bones.

Sauces to Dehydrate

Some sauces lend themselves to dehydrating to leather. Do not dehydrate sauces that have a high fat content or contain dairy products. Some thick commercial sauces won't dry out completely due to the presence of oil and are not recommended for long-term storage. You can make many sauces at home and omit the oils. After dehydrating, if the leather sticks to the tray, try freezing it for an hour. It should become brittle enough to pry from the tray. Dehydrated sauces are easy to transport in their thickened state and can be appropriate for short term use. Dehydrate homemade versions without oil to a brittle state and grind into a powder.

- Tomato salsa (red)
- Tomatillo salsa (green)
- BBQ sauce
- Ketchup
- Hoisin sauce
- Chinese black bean sauce
- Teriyaki sauce
- Satay sauce
- Chutney
- Costa Rican Lizano Salsa

I used dehydrated fresh salsa throughout my JMT hike, which means it lasted at least six weeks between the time I prepared it and it was consumed. However, we had some left over after the trip and after several months it looked suspect, as if it might have either oxidized or possibly developed mold. I threw it out and now store my leathers separately from the rest of the meal in the tiny "pill pouches" (previously described).

Salsa on a drying rack prior to being dehydrated

Standard Condiments

I recommend bringing a standard set of condiments that will last the entire trip. These are separate from the spices included in individual meals. I used to bring more but now I just bring salt, pepper, red pepper flakes and olive oil. I've found that among those four, even the most bland, boring, dismal meal can be salvaged. Experiment to find what works for you--perhaps some oregano, basil, lemon pepper, chili powder or seasoning blend you use at home will enhance your trail food.

Bring a good amount of salt. Hikers can lose a lot of electrolytes and often need more salt that they expect. The recipes in the next chapter have low amounts of salt since everyone's needs are different and it's preferable to add salt as desired. For reference, a standard salt packet that you would get from a restaurant contains ⅛ teaspoon of salt.

Suggested condiments:

- Salt
- Black pepper
- Red pepper flakes
- Herb seasoning blend
- Olive oil

Chapter 11: Recipes with "buy or dry" ingredients

This is a collection of base recipes that you can build on and modify to create a variety of meals. These recipes are constructed around ingredients you buy (usually freeze-dried) or dry at home with a dehydrator. Feel free to mix and match variations of basic ingredients to suit your taste (brown rice vs white rice, black bean vs white bean, beef vs sausage, etc.).

Generally, home-dehydrated foods can be substituted for freeze-dried ingredients (e.g. dehydrated ground meat, vegetables and fruit can be substituted for freeze-dried). Freeze-dried is lighter, dryer and retains more nutrients though home dehydrated is less expensive. Decide which works for you based on your budget, equipment and time. Refer back to the Food Safety section in Chapter 2 for information about food safety, storage and shelf-stability.

Follow this link to The Hungry Spork Data Sheets (bit.ly/HungrySporkDataSheets) for detailed nutrition information for each recipe.

General Tips

Recipe Details

- When the recipe says "cooked and dehydrated," it means the finished product. Measure for the recipe after cooking and dehydrating. Therefore, "½ cup lentils cooked and dehydrated" means that you've cooked up a big batch of lentils, dehydrated them and are now scooping ½ cup of the dehydrated product into your trail recipe.

- Recipes are for one serving. For comparison, a typical commercial freeze-dried meal contains about 4.8 ounce. Aim for about 5-7 ounce per serving, depending on expected appetite. Go a little heavier for bigger appetites, such as teenagers, many men or anyone after a particularly grueling day.
- Look at the calorie count for each recipe. If you have a big appetite, consider doubling the recipe or adding more meat or starch to increase the calories. Freeze-dried sausage crumbles offer the most calories at 280 calories for ½ cup. Compare that to freeze-dried chicken at 120 calories for ½ cup.

Sources

- See Chapter 10 for spice blend recipes and note the standard condiment recommendations for trail staples to bring.
- Refer to the Appendix to locate brands and sources for freeze-dried foods and less common foods such as coconut milk powder, umami seasoning or organic ramen.

Substitutions

- Most of the meals contain meat, but vegetarians can eliminate the meat and add veggies, legumes, grains, nuts, seeds, dehydrated tofu, dehydrated tempeh or textured vegetable protein (TVP).
- If you don't eat beef or don't like lamb, substitute other meats or protein sources such as chicken, turkey or tuna.
- Any kind of noodle can be substituted for the Asian noodles. Be aware that calorie counts can vary substantially so read the label. Thin noodles such as ramen, rice or soba noodles will rehydrate easily, even in cold water. Thicker noodles may need to be simmered at camp or cooked and dehydrated at home.

- When fruit is called for I often use freeze-dried grapes because they don't contain any additives, are lighter and retain more nutrients than dried. In place of freeze-dried fruit the more commonly found raisins, dried cranberries or dried apricots can be substituted. Many dried fruits are treated with sulfur dioxide as a preservative, which some people are sensitive to. If you see dried fruit with a vibrant color that is similar to fresh, it probably was treated with sulfur. Naturally dried fruit with no sulfur is darker.

Additions

- Add up to a tablespoon each of chia seeds and flax seeds to any of these meals to boost flavor, texture, protein and fat. Instant quinoa flakes, a good source of protein, can also be added to many meals, especially ones with mashed potatoes.
- Olive oil is included in each recipe to provide additional calories and flavor. I've included one tablespoon in calorie counts. If you are looking for ways to increase calories and fat, use more. Some people can tolerate two tablespoons or more. On the other hand, you can omit the oil or reduce the amount if you prefer. Other oils or ghee (clarified butter) can be substituted.
- It's convenient to carry one type of oil, such as a mild olive oil, but there are more flavorful options. Coconut oil or a touch of sesame oil can jazz up Asian dishes, and lemon oil provides a bright flavor for tabbouleh, marinara and Indian dishes. For strongly flavored oils, such as sesame, use a small amount along with a neutral-flavored oil. Residual coconut oil can be more difficult to clean from rehydration bags.
- Bouillon has been omitted from recipes because the commercial products contain MSG or MSG-like substances that some people are sensitive to. Homemade bouillon can enhance gravies, soups and many of the recipes in this chapter. See the

recipe for *Homemade Poultry Bouillon* in the previous chapter. If you normally consume commercial bouillon or if you have the homemade version you may want to add small amounts (½ to 1 teaspoon) to some of the recipes, including the Asian recipes, beef stew, grits and more.

- It's easy to add water if a meal is too thick but it's impossible to remove it. Therefore, start with ½-¾ cup of water to rehydrate initially. Usually you will need to add up to ½ cup more. Your meal will be warmer if you add the additional hot water immediately before eating.
- Likewise, you can add more salt but you can't take it away. Add salt to the recipes to suit your taste, remembering that you will likely need more salt than you're used to. As a reference point, a standard salt packet from a restaurant contains ⅛ teaspoon of salt. I've added up to ½ teaspoon of salt to the recipes and not found it to taste particularly salty. Be aware of other ingredients you're using that contain salt (e.g. freeze-dried sausage crumbles or bouillon) and adjust accordingly, especially if they were not part of the original recipe.

Altitude

- At low elevations foods may rehydrate in 10 minutes while at the lofty elevation of the High Sierra it may take 15-20 minutes or longer to fully soften some foods.

Nutrition

- See The Hungry Spork Data Sheets (bit.ly/HungrySporkDataSheets) for detailed nutrition information.

Oatmeal with Fixings

Oatmeal is a class breakfast food but can also make a tummy-friendly dinner. Though plain instant oatmeal doesn't have many calories or nutrients, supplementing with various topping choices solves that problem. Think of it as a starchy vehicle for the good stuff.

Ingredients

2 packages instant oatmeal-plain
1 tablespoon hazelnuts
1 tablespoon hemp hearts
1 tablespoon raisins
1 tablespoon brown sugar
1 teaspoon roasted flax seeds
1 teaspoon chia seeds
1 tablespoon full fat powdered milk

At home

Combine all the dry ingredients into a bag.

In camp

Add enough hot water to cover.
Stir well to moisten throughout.
Rehydrate for a few minutes until softened.
Add additional cup of hot water if desired.

1 serving
Calories 416; Carbohydrate 71 g; Protein 15 g; Fat 25 g; Sodium 186 mg

Variations

- Substitute other hot cereals from different grains such as wheat, rice or corn (grits).
- Cereal topping choices are endless. Here are a few.
    - Chopped dried dates

- Dried cranberry
- Raisins
- Flax seeds
- Chia seeds
- Hemp seeds
- Hazelnuts
- Coconut flakes or chips
- Chocolate
- Cocoa
- Almonds
- Walnuts
- Pecans
- Oat bran
- Wheat bran
- Banana chips
- Dried apples
- Dried apricots
- Brown sugar
- Maple sugar
- Honey crystals
- Cinnamon
- Ghee
- Olive oil
- Coconut oil
- Powdered butter
- Dried meats
- Dried vegetables
- Aged fresh or freeze-dried cheese
- Protein powder
- Powdered peanut butter

Simple Healthy Ramen

When your appetite is suppressed due to the effects of altitude or physical exhaustion, ramen is easy to get down. It also makes a good hot lunch on a chilly day if you have time to heat water. The variations are endless with additional veggies or meats or variations in the spices. It can be a noodle dish if you use less water or a soup if you add more.

Ramen spice packets are often loaded with MSG. If you avoid MSG, discard the spice packet and try Asian Ramen Blend in the previous chapter. Many people avoid the inexpensive ubiquitous ramen noodles found in many supermarkets because they contain preservatives such as tertiary-butyl hydroquinone (TBHQ). Healthier options can be found if you search for organic noodles, scrutinize the ingredient list and make your own seasoning. Koyo Organic Ramen is a better option than many brands found in supermarkets as it has no additives, preservatives or MSG. Lotus Forbidden Rice Ramen is gluten-free, vegan and is uniquely black in color, giving a rich brown broth. Happy Pho from Star Anise Foods is made with brown rice and contains no MSG, but the noodles soften more if boiled—use if cooking with a pot. Note that some of the specialty ramen blocks are fairly small. Use a whole block of these even if the package states that it's two servings.

Ingredients

1 serving of ramen (½ or 1 block, depending on brand; discard the spice blend)
¼ cup freeze-dried peas
3 dried shiitake mushrooms, sliced thinly
1 teaspoon Umami Dust Seasoning (optional, see note below)
½ teaspoon Asian Ramen Blend (Chapter 10)
1 teaspoon minced dried onion
Salt (optional if you use Umami Dust Seasoning, which contains salt)

Trail Staple

1 tablespoon olive oil

At home
Combine all the dry ingredients into a bag.

In camp

Add enough hot water to cover. Start with 1 cup.
Add olive oil.
Stir well to moisten throughout.
Rehydrate for 10-20 minutes until softened.
Add up to 1 additional cup of hot water to taste if desired.

1 serving
Calories 416; Carbohydrate 62 g; Protein 12 g; Fat 15 g; Sodium 947 mg (with 1 Koyo Organic Ramen block)
Variant: Calories 586; Carbohydrate 49 g; Protein 14 g; Fat 28 g; Sodium 297 mg (With 1 Nissen Ramen block, 1/8 tsp salt and no Umami Dust Seasoning)

Variations

- This is a vegetarian dish. Vegetarians can add dehydrated tofu, dehydrated tempeh or textured vegetable protein (TVP).
- Rice noodles, instant soba noodles or other noodles can be substituted for the ramen. If you're using a thick noodle you may need to experiment to see if it will rehydrate without simmering, otherwise you may need to cook the noodles at home and dehydrate. Be aware that the calorie count may be substantially reduced with other kinds of noodles.
- Add freeze-dried chicken, diced salami, tuna from a foil packet, salmon jerky or other meat for a more robust meal. As is, it's a light meal; therefore 1 tablespoon of olive oil is recommended to add additional calories.

- If you're simmering in a pot you can add dehydrated eggs.
- Add any number of freeze-dried or dehydrated veggies including green onion, shredded cabbage, broccoli, carrots, red bell pepper, etc.
- Black or white sesame seeds can be added.
- Coconut oil can be substituted for olive oil.
- Substitute 1 teaspoon of porcini, shiitake or morel mushroom powder for Umami Dust Seasoning if you limit sodium and avoid any possibility of MSG. Umami Dust Seasoning contains salt and "natural flavoring," which may or may not contain MSG.
- PoLoKu Mushroom Seasoning (1 teaspoon) is another possible addition that will increase flavor and sodium but it's ingredients are unknown and may contain MSG.
- Soy sauce from individual packets can be used, along with Sriracha sauce for more heat.

Reviewer notes

One reviewer tested this recipe with her family. They found it a bit bland, so they used another ¼ teaspoon of the Umami Dust Seasoning (total 1¼ teaspoon) in 2 cups of broth. They still thought the broth was flat so they added ½ teaspoon of mushroom seasoning. This did the trick for them. They further experimented with adding ½ tablespoon peanut butter, saying that "it took the broth to a different yummy level." [Author note: I tried the PoLoKu Mushroom Seasoning and it did give the ramen a nice bump in flavor. However, since the Umami Dust Seasoning contains salt and so does the PoLoKu Mushroom Seasoning, so I did not include it in the recipe.]

Chinese Cashew Chicken Noodles

This is the only recipe that calls for any liquid to be carried separately. The dressing is so good that there is no dried substitute. I bring the dressing in a tiny Nalgene bottle and wash it out after using it. Then I let the bottle roll around in the bottom of my pack until the trip is over.

Ingredients

1 serving of ramen (½ or 1 block, depending on brand) or 2 ounces of other Asian noodles (discard the spice blend)
½ cup freeze-dried chicken
1 tablespoon chopped cashews
¼ cup dried cabbage
⅛ cup freeze-dried broccoli
1 teaspoon minced dried onion
1 teaspoon *furikake* (sesame with seaweed flakes) or roasted sesame seeds
1 teaspoon roasted flax seeds
1 teaspoon chia seeds
Cilantro-fresh or dehydrated (optional)

Dressing:

2 teaspoons soy sauce
1 teaspoon rice vinegar (or other vinegar)
½ teaspoon of sugar or other sweetener such as honey or agave syrup
⅛ teaspoon sesame oil
Pinch of hot pepper flakes (optional)

Tail Staple

1 tablespoon olive oil

At home

Combine all the dry ingredients into a bag.

Mix the vinegar, sugar, salt, sesame oil and soy sauce in a bowl. Stir until sugar is dissolved. Place in a small, non-leak bottle.

In camp

Add enough hot water to cover. Start with ½-1 cup.
Add olive oil.
Stir well to moisten throughout.
Rehydrate for 10-20 minutes until softened.
Add more hot water to taste if desired.
Add the dressing and mix thoroughly.

Yield: 1 serving
Calories 586; Carbohydrate 71 g; Protein 40 g; Fat 18 g; Sodium 769 mg

Variations

- This can be a vegetarian dish if the chicken is omitted. Vegetarians can add dehydrated tofu, dehydrated tempeh or textured vegetable protein (TVP).
- Rice noodles, instant soba noodles or other noodles can be substituted for the ramen. If you're using a thick noodle you may need to experiment to see if it will rehydrate without simmering, otherwise you may need to cook the noodles at home and dehydrate. Be aware that the calorie count may be substantially reduced with other kinds of noodles.
- If you like seaweed, add 3 sheets of roasted seaweed snack
- Coconut oil can be substituted for olive oil.
- If you like spicy food, bring individual Sriracha sauce packets for more robust flavor.

Reviewer notes

There are no official reviewer notes for this version as the recipe was completely revamped. However, feedback from a previous version of the recipe included using coconut sugar and raw organic honey in place of sugar, coconut aminos as a gluten-free substitute for soy sauce and using bagged cole slaw mix for the cabbage. One reviewer loved the crunch of the nuts and seeds. She would have used sesame oil next time for more flavor and some dried cranberries for some tang.

I (the author) made it twice in the current version and loved it; so did my husband. I made it with freeze-dried chicken and it was a hearty dinner. I tried it with coconut oil but since it is a solid in cool temperatures I found that it was easier to use olive oil during the rehydration process. The coconut oil stuck to the inside of the container and made a real mess on the inside surface of the reusable plastic bag I was rehydrating in, requiring quite a bit of hot water to clean it off.

Indonesian Chicken Noodles

We love Asian flavors so anything with coconut cream powder is a winner for us. If you like stronger flavors use the larger amount of the Thai Spice Blend. See my comments about ramen in the Simple Healthier Ramen recipe above.

Ingredients

1 serving of ramen (½ or 1 block, depending on brand) or 2 ounce of other Asian noodles (discard the spice blend)
½ cup freeze-dried chicken
⅛ cup chopped peanuts
3 dried shiitake mushrooms, sliced thinly
3 tablespoons mixed freeze-dried mixed vegetables
¼ cup dried shredded cabbage
2 tablespoons peanut butter powder
1 tablespoon coconut cream powder
1 teaspoon roasted flax seeds
1 teaspoon chia seeds
1-2 teaspoons Thai Spice Blend (Chapter 10)
1 packet (a bit more than ⅛ teaspoon or 0.8 gram) of lemon powder
⅛ teaspoon salt

Trail Staple

1 tablespoon olive oil

At home

Mix dry ingredients together in a zip top baggie. Keep the nuts separate in a small baggie.

In camp

Add enough hot water to cover. Start with ½-1 cup.

Add olive oil.
Stir well to moisten throughout.
Rehydrate for 10-20 minutes until softened.
Add more hot water to taste if desired.
Add the peanuts.

Yield: 1 serving
Calories 912; Carbohydrate 93 g; Protein 37 g; Fat 48 g; Sodium 537 mg

Variations

- This can be a vegetarian dish if the chicken is omitted. Vegetarians can add dehydrated tofu, dehydrated tempeh or textured vegetable protein (TVP).
- Rice noodles, instant soba noodles or other noodles can be substituted for the ramen. If you're using a thick or dense noodle you may need to experiment to see if it will rehydrate without simmering, otherwise you may need to cook the noodles at home and dehydrate.
- Macadamia nuts may be substituted for peanuts. Indonesian recipes often use kemiri (candlenut) nuts, which are similar to macadamia nuts.
- Dried lemon zest or lime powder can be substituted for lemon powder.
- Coconut oil can be substituted for olive oil.
- On short trips, bring a small amount of *kecap manis* (sweet Indonesian soy sauce). The thick sauce can be dehydrated to leather. A dash of brown sugar could substitute as a dry ingredient.
- If you like it hot, bring some *sambal ulek*, a hot pepper condiment, or Sriracha sauce packets. Authentic Indonesian food can be very hot and spicy.

Reviewer notes

One reviewer garnished with soy sauce and said it was good. She experimented with "*mai fun*" noodles, which ended up not needing to be pre-cooked and dehydrated; they rehydrated fine out of the package. She used a pack of Justin's peanut butter instead of the powder and used sesame oil instead of olive oil. She added too much water on the trail and found it too watery. She said 1 cup would have been about right. She really liked it and so did her husband.

Another reviewer said the spices were perfect, except that she halved the ginger due to personal preference. She used glass noodles, omitted the red pepper and mushrooms and added 1 tablespoon of dried onion. She added a bit more water than called for. "Really enjoyed the combination of coconut powder and peanut butter. Yum!"

A third reviewer used 2 ounces of Annie Chun's Pad Thai Brown Rice Noodles and tested two samples, finding that they did not need to be cooked and dehydrated; it rehydrated fine out of the box. She dehydrated canned chicken and raw or steamed veggies. Overall, she liked the dish but she prefers more protein and veggies with fewer noodles. She likes her meals soupy and used nearly two cups of water to rehydrate on the trail. "This recipe not only smelled good to me but tasted so good! I will be making it again in the future."

A fourth reviewer thought this needed more spice and used 1.5 teaspoon instead of 1 teaspoon. She also increased the coconut cream powder to 1.5 tablespoons and 3 tablespoons of peanut butter powder. She used 2 ounces brown rice vermicelli and substituted almonds for the nuts. She added 1 tablespoon vegan chicken broth powder, ½ teaspoon of dried green onions and ½ teaspoon dried cilantro. She brought an individual packet of soy sauce to add at the end. She used about 1¼ cup of water to rehydrate on the trail. "This was one of my top 2 recipes! Wanted to take it every trip."

A fifth reviewer did a vegetarian variation, just using noodles and nuts (no meat). She used 2 tablespoons of powdered coconut milk. She felt it needed a little sweetness so she added ½ teaspoon of brown sugar and liked the addition. She used ½ cup of water. "I love the sauce it made. Very creamy and flavorful. It was very filling and I couldn't finish the entire bowl. Very satisfying."

A sixth reviewer said, "This was one of my favorites. I would definitely eat this every trip." She thought it made too much food for a non-through hiker and would reduce the serving size by ¼ next time.

Thai Curry Chicken and Rice

This is becoming one of our favorite trail meals. The coconut cream power is what makes it, so don't skip that ingredient.

A couple of reviewers found this recipe to be too bland with 1 teaspoon of the Thai spice blend but others liked the original recipe so I modified it to include 1-2 teaspoons. If you like spicy food, ramp it up with some Sriracha sauce packets. I personally have had trouble with home-dehydrated rice not completely softening, as some of the reviewers did. I now use freeze-dried rice for better results though others report success with instant rice.

Thai Curry Chicken and Rice after rehydration on the trail

Ingredients

½ cup freeze-dried, dehydrated or instant rice (brown or white)
¼ cup freeze-dried chicken
1 tablespoon chopped cashews

¼ cup freeze-dried peas
⅛ cup dried carrots
1 tablespoon coconut cream powder
1 teaspoon minced dried onion
1 teaspoon roasted flax
1 teaspoon chia seeds
1-2 teaspoons Thai Spice Blend (Chapter 10)
1 packet (a bit more than ⅛ teaspoon or 0.8 gram) of lemon powder
⅛ teaspoon salt

Trail Staple

1 tablespoon olive oil

At home

Mix dry ingredients together in a zip-top baggie.

In camp

Add enough hot water to cover. Start with ½-1 cup.
Add olive oil.
Stir well to moisten throughout.
Rehydrate for 10-20 minutes until softened.
Add more hot water to taste if desired.

Yield: 1 serving
Calories 629; Carbohydrate 54 g; Protein 39 g; Fat 28 g; Sodium 374 mg

Variations

- This can be a vegetarian dish if the chicken is omitted. Vegetarians can add dehydrated tofu, dehydrated tempeh or textured vegetable protein (TVP).
- Dehydrated beef or foil-pouch fish (tuna or salmon) can be substituted for the chicken.

- For a short trip, bring some fresh cilantro, or dehydrate it for extra flavor.
- Dried lemon zest or lime powder can be substituted for lemon powder.
- Coconut oil can be substituted for olive oil.
- If you like spicy food, bring individual Sriracha sauce packets.

Reviewer notes

One reviewer reduced the ginger and added curry powder, as well as increasing the coconut milk powder by 1 teaspoon. She used brown rice and tried both coconut oil and sesame oil, "each were great." She needed a little more water.

Another reviewer used a mix of white and wild rice but reported that the wild rice didn't completely rehydrate. She used a vegan "chicken" broth powder. She also said that a little more water was needed.

A third reviewer found the spices to be mild so she doubled the amount of Thai spice blend to 2 teaspoon (I modified the recipe to 1-2 teaspoons). She used ⅔ cup of white rice (that's ⅔ cup cooked, prior to dehydrating). She didn't measure the hot water for hydrating the meal; instead she just poured the hot water in the bag to cover the meal, plus a bit more. She found the serving size to be too large, rehydrating about ⅔ of the serving and holding back ⅓. She said, "I really liked this meal a lot. It looked good, smelled good and was very tummy friendly." Her friend thought it was one of the best things she had eaten on the trail.

A fourth reviewer used 1 teaspoon of the Thai spice blend and found the recipe to be too bland. She would bring red pepper flakes or Sriracha sauce next time. She used instant brown rice but found that the rice didn't fully rehydrate even with a longer steeping time.

Indian Chicken, Lentils and Quinoa

I lived in Southeast Asia as a child and grew up eating curries and lentils. I love them but find that the strong curry flavor can be too much if my appetite is suppressed. Therefore, I use restraint with the spices. I've also heard that some people have had their entire bear canister smell like curry so you might want to double bag this recipe. I include it because so many people mention curry dishes among their favorite and it truly is tasty if you like curry. This was a favorite among the testers.

Cooked quinoa before dehydration

Ingredients

½ cup lentils, cooked and dehydrated
¼ cup quinoa, cooked and dehydrated
½ cup freeze-dried chicken
2 tablespoon freeze-dried grapes or raisins
¼ cup freeze-dried broccoli

4 slices dried tomato
1 teaspoon minced dried onion
1 teaspoon roasted flax
1 teaspoon chia seeds
1 teaspoon powdered butter
1 teaspoon of Indian Spice Blend (Chapter 10)
⅛ teaspoon salt

Trail Staple

1 tablespoon olive oil

At home

Mix everything together in a zip top baggie.

In camp

Add enough hot water to cover. Start with ½-1 cup.
Add olive oil.
Stir well to moisten throughout.
Rehydrate for 10-20 minutes until softened.
Add more hot water to taste if desired.

Yield: 1 serving
Calories 720; Carbohydrate 83 g; Protein 45 g; Fat 24 g; Sodium 391 mg

Variations

- This can be a vegetarian dish if the chicken is omitted. Nuts, seeds, dehydrated tofu, dehydrated tempeh or textured vegetable protein (TVP) can be added.
- Rice can be substituted for the quinoa and/or lentils.
- Quinoa flakes can be used instead of cooked and dehydrated quinoa though the texture will be different. Whole quinoa retains a bit of crunch while the flakes are soft.
- Coconut oil can be substituted for olive oil.

- Chutney can transform this meal. Dehydrate chutney to leather and add to recipe when it is rehydrating on the trail. On short trips, bring a small container of chutney. Pita or tortillas can stand in for *naan* bread.

Reviewer notes

One reviewer likes a lot of spice so she slightly increased the curry powder in the Indian Spice Blend and added 1 tablespoon of coconut milk powder. She found richer flavor with sun-dried tomatoes instead of plain tomatoes. She also used coconut oil. She used slightly more water and rehydrated 20 minutes to allow the lentils to fully rehydrate. She said, "Really liked this, particularly the fact that it contained quinoa" and gave it a top score.

A second reviewer thought the Indian Spice Blend was "just right." She used sun-dried tomatoes and 1 tablespoon of vegan chicken bouillon. She used a cup of water and might add a bit more hot water just before eating. She said, "One of my top two, also every friend that wanted a bite of this loved it!"

Another reviewer said the spices were good, adding, "Loved it but my hiking partner did not care for it (not a diverse eater). She thought the serving size was too much, saying that about 75% would be perfect for her.

Moroccan Tabbouleh

I love this dish because it stands out from the typical backpacking fare. It can be made with beef or chicken though lamb is a favored meat in Middle Eastern cuisine. Sometimes I mix ½ dehydrated ground lamb with ½ dehydrated ground turkey. Because the lamb flavor is not as neutral as other recipes, this is one that I include sparingly to break up the monotony as its distinctive flavors are very welcome.

The sodium content will be significantly reduced if you dehydrate your own beef. Freeze-dried beef varies greatly in sodium.

Ingredients

¼ cup tabbouleh (bulgur) or couscous
¼ cup freeze-dried beef or dehydrated lamb
2 tablespoons sliced almonds
2 tablespoons freeze-dried grapes
4 slices dried tomato
2 teaspoons dried or freeze-dried chopped carrots
1 teaspoon minced dried onion
1 teaspoon roasted flax
1 teaspoon chia seeds
1 teaspoon of Moroccan Spice Blend (Chapter 10)
1 packet (0.8 gram) of lemon powder or dried lemon zest
Salt (optional as freeze-dried beef may contain salt)

Trail Staple

1 tablespoon olive oil

At home

Combine all the dry ingredients into a bag.

In camp

Add enough hot water to cover. Start with ½-1 cup.
Add olive oil.
Stir well to moisten throughout.
Rehydrate for 10-20 minutes until softened.
Add more hot water to taste if desired.

Yield: 1 serving
Calories 625; Carbohydrate 44 g; Protein 27 g; Fat 40 g; Sodium 618 mg

Variations

- This can be a vegetarian dish if the meat is omitted. Nuts, seeds, dehydrated tofu, dehydrated tempeh or textured vegetable protein (TVP) can be added.
- Dried cranberries, apricot bits or raisins may be substituted for grapes.
- Dried limes, which are a staple in Middle Eastern recipes, can be substituted for the lemon powder for an earthier, smokier flavoring. Dried lemon or lime zest or lime powder can also be substituted for lemon powder.
- Lemon oil can be added on the trail.

Reviewer notes

A reviewer gave this recipe a top score and said it "was her favorite" of the recipes she tried, saying that "it was different than other food we usually have when backpacking. This will definitely go into our regular rotation." She used a packaged Tabbouleh mix in a box, dehydrated ground beef and dried tart cherries instead of grapes.

Italian Marinara, Sausage and Orzo Pasta

This is a standby staple meal. It always tastes good and we can eat it every few days without complaint. I vary the meat and veggies a bit so it doesn't taste the same each time.

You can use the tomato powder listed in the ingredients or you can dehydrate your own.

Ingredients

¼ cup tomato powder
½ cup orzo, cooked and dehydrated
¼ cup freeze-dried sausage
4 slices dried tomato
1 tablespoon freeze-dried cheddar cheese
1 teaspoon freeze-dried parmesan cheese
1 teaspoon Italian Spice Blend (optional, depending on how robust the marinara sauce is) (Chapter 10)
1 teaspoon minced dried onion
⅛ teaspoon red pepper flakes
Salt (optional as freeze-dried sausage may contain salt)
Black pepper to taste

Trail Staple

1 tablespoon olive oil

At home

Combine the rest of the dry ingredients into a bag.

In camp

Add enough hot water to cover the dry ingredients. Start with ½-1 cup.

Add olive oil.
Stir well to moisten throughout.
Add hot water to the bag.
Rehydrate for 10-20 minutes until softened.
Add more hot water to taste if desired.

Yield: 1 serving
Calories 851; Carbohydrate 106 g; Protein 37 g; Fat 34 g; Sodium 691 mg

Variations

- This can be a vegetarian dish if the meat is omitted. Textured vegetable protein could be substituted.
- Dehydrated marinara or tomato paste can be substituted for tomato powder.
    - Make your own mild marinara sauce or use a commercial product. Simmer uncovered on the stove to thicken the sauce to a paste. Add a little red wine (optional). When the sauce thickens, remove from heat and let it cool. Spread on dehydrator trays with "fruit leather" liners. This can also be done in the oven using the lowest temperature.
    - Use one cup of liquid marinara sauce dehydrated to leather (about ¼ cup or 1 ounce leather) per serving. Sauces can vary quite a bit so if it's too tomato-y, use less.
    - Shred or cut the marinara leather into tiny bits. If the meal is to be stored long term, it would be prudent to store the leather in a small "pill pouch" since the leathers are not as dry as other ingredients.
    - On the trail, add hot water to the bag with marinara sauce and gently knead it to reconstitute the sauce.
- Farro (an ancient wheat grain also known as emmer), cooked and dehydrated, can be substituted for orzo pasta.

- An interesting variation on pasta is polenta. Use instant polenta in a tube. Slice, fry and dehydrate the "polenta pucks." Rehydrate in water to cover. They will remain chewy but can be a nice change of pace. Because of the oil, fried polenta is suitable for short term trips of up to a few weeks.
- Substitute freeze-dried beef or dehydrated ground turkey instead of sausage.
- Add red wine to marinara sauce before rehydrating for a richer flavor.

Reviewer notes

One reviewer used a simple version of spices and may have added some commercial Italian Seasoning to make up for not using the full spice recipe. She liked the ingredients, using gluten-free pasta and homemade sauce dehydrated to leather. She packed the leather in a separate pouch. She couldn't find gluten-free orzo so she used spiral noodles successfully. She has a "really good appetite despite altitude" but was not hungry after eating a full serving. She used ¾-1 cup of water. She, her husband and friend all loved it and would definitely make it again. The portions were good for all of them.

Another reviewer tried this with both orzo and angel hair pasta and both worked well. She used a bit less water than called for. She said, "This is a favorite I will make again and again."

A third reviewer tried angel hair pasta but found it a bit mushy. She increased the cheese to 1 tablespoon each. She used at least a cup of water. She said it was almost too much food each time.

Cajun Chicken, Sausage and Rice

Feedback from the testers was all over the board on the original recipe and we were, too. My husband loved it and I thought it was pretty good, but it needed work after the first round of testing. The main issue was that it used to taste more Italian, though it did have some strong fans. The recipe and spice blend has since been revamped.

The freeze-dried rice works better for me though others have had success with dehydrated rice. Mine never seems to fully rehydrate and was overly chewy, but the freeze-dried rice is good. I also like the dehydrated farro variant.

Ingredients

¼ cup tomato powder
½ cup freeze-dried, dehydrated or instant rice (brown or white)
¼ cup freeze-dried sausage
½ cup freeze-dried chicken
4 slices dried tomato
2 tablespoons freeze-dried bell pepper
2 tablespoons dried chopped celery (optional)
1 teaspoon minced dried onion
1 teaspoon Cajun Spice Blend (Chapter 10)
1 packet (a bit more than ⅛ teaspoon or 0.8 gram) of lemon powder
Salt (optional as sausage contains salt)
Black pepper to taste

Trail Staple

1 tablespoon olive oil

At home

Combine all the dry ingredients into a bag.
Mix dry ingredients together in a zip-top baggie.

<u>In camp</u>

Add enough hot water to cover the dry ingredients. Start with ½-1 cup.
Add olive oil.
Stir well to moisten throughout.
Rehydrate for 10-20 minutes until softened.
Combine the sauce with the rest of the ingredients
Add more hot water to taste if desired.

Yield: 1 serving
Calories 672; Carbohydrate 65 g; Protein 42 g; Fat 30 g; Sodium 659 mg (without added salt)

Cajun Chicken, Sausage and Rice (with green beans, a variation)

Variations

- This can be a vegetarian dish if the meat is omitted. Textured vegetable protein could be substituted.
- Dehydrated tomato paste can be substituted for the tomato powder. Use ¼ small can (1.5 ounce of 6 ounce can) of tomato paste dehydrated to leather (about 9 grams of leather per serving). There are two options for dehydrating the tomato paste.
    - Option 1, spread tomato paste on dehydrator trays with liners and dry.
    - Option 2, sauté tomato paste in a small amount of oil, add fresh or dried vegetables, spices, lemon powder or squirt of fresh lemon juice and dehydrate. Because of the oil this method is not ideal for very long-term storage, but the flavors will be more rich and earthy.
- An Italian version can be made by substituting dehydrated marinara sauce (See "Variations" in the *Italian Sausage and Orzo Pasta* recipe for directions) for tomato paste and Italian spices instead of Cajun spices.
- Farro (an ancient wheat grain also known as emmer), cooked and dehydrated, can be substituted for rice.
- Include dried okra "chips" or dehydrate your own for an authentic touch, or substitute green beans.
- Dried lemon zest can be substituted for lemon powder.
- A packet of hot sauce (e.g. Cholula® or Tabasco®) worked some magic with this dish.
- The photo shows dried shrimp, which was tested and found to add nothing so it was omitted from the recipe.

Reviewer notes

A reviewer who tasted the current version of the recipe appreciated the flavor of the plain tomato versus the previous version that used marinara sauce. She used 1 tablespoon of tomato powder instead of dehydrated tomato paste and added 1 ½ teaspoons of vegan chicken broth with good results. I have since revised the recipe to include ¼ cup of tomato powder, but if that's too tomato-y for you, just cut back.

Note from author: *The following reviews were for an earlier version that was called Jambalaya but tasted more Italian (similar to the variation using Italian marinara). The recipe and spices have since been revised.*

One reviewer used fire roasted tomatoes instead of slices and used 1 cup of water to rehydrate. She said, "I love this" and gave it a top score.

Another reviewer omitted the meat and used brown rice. She used one cup of water but felt it could have used more. "Flavor is good. Very saucy, borders on the side of Italian vs Cajun."

A third reviewer said, "Loved this and would make it again, for sure." She shared it with PCT thru-hikers who liked the original spice blend. They thought the meal had more flavor than anything they had tasted on the trail so far, though they didn't think it tasted Cajun. The reviewer thought the portion was large and that 75% would probably be adequate for women hikers, thought the PCT hikers were very appreciative.

A fourth reviewer, whose husband is from New Orleans, thought it didn't have the typical "rich" flavor of authentic Jambalaya, almost certainly due to the lack of traditional roux. She added dehydrated celery and okra and used instant rice. She added extra water. She said, "Not one of my favorites, but that is probably my own preference for Jambalaya made with the traditional roux," and gave it a neutral score.

A fifth reviewer doesn't normally eat Jambalaya and didn't care for it. It was to tomato-y for her and thought maybe it wasn't spicy enough. She used the Cajun Spice Blend and used smoked paprika, her regular classic tomato-basil marinara sauce and instant brown rice.

Beef Stew with Mashed Sweet Potato

This is full of rich beef flavor that pairs well with the sweet potato. That, along with the smooth texture of the mashed potato and beef gravy, makes it pure comfort food. We look forward to this dish a lot and I almost can't make enough dehydrated sweet potato bark.

There is a lot of confusion around sweet potatoes vs yams. I use the tuber with an orange skin and deep orange or yellow flesh, sometimes labeled Jewel or Garnet Yam. Either yams or sweet potatoes can be used.

The sodium content will be significantly reduced if you dehydrate your own beef. Freeze-dried beef varies greatly in sodium. Commercial gravy mixes are generally made with a lot of additives, including MSG and related substances, but it is difficult to replicate the packaged gravy powders. See "Variations" for suggestions for alternatives, including the Mushroom Gravy recipe in previous chapter.

Mashed yam (front) on the drying rack (along with quinoa (left) and salsa)

Ingredients

½ cup sweet potato bark (½ large sweet potato, boiled, mashed and dehydrated) or freeze-dried sweet potato
¼ cup freeze-dried or dehydrated ground beef
¼ cup freeze-dried peas
2 tablespoons freeze-dried cheddar cheese
1 tablespoon full fat powdered milk
½ tablespoon powdered butter
1 teaspoon Italian Spice Blend (Chapter 10)
Salt (optional as freeze-dried beef and powdered gravy mix may contain salt)
Black pepper to taste

Gravy:
2 teaspoons brown gravy mix (1 part commercial gravy mix to 4 parts water or homemade-see Chapter 10)

Trail Staple

1 tablespoon olive oil

At home

Combine all the dry ingredients into a bag. If you want to create a layered meal, package the mashed potatoes in one bag, the gravy mix in a small zip-top bag, and the rest of the dry ingredients in yet another bag.

In camp

If packaged together, add enough hot water to cover. Start with ½-1 cup.
Add olive oil.
Stir well to moisten throughout.
Rehydrate for 10-20 minutes until softened.
Add more hot water to taste if desired.

If packaged separately, add ½ cup hot water and olive oil to the bag with the meat.
Add water to cover the sweet potato bark in the separate bag.
Rehydrate for 10-20 minutes until softened.
Add a small amount of hot water to the bag with gravy mix.
Just before serving, empty the potatoes into a bowl. Add meat to the bowl.
Top with gravy.

Yield: 1 serving
Calories 640; Carbohydrate 33 g; Protein 33 g; Fat 41 g; Sodium 714 mg

Variations

- This could be a vegetarian dish if textured vegetable protein were substituted for the beef.
- Freeze-dried sweet potato can be used instead of dehydrated.
- Use ½ cup instant mashed potatoes instead of sweet potato bark.
- Substitute freeze-dried green beans or other veggies instead of peas.
- If you are sensitive to even tiny amounts of MSG, substitute Mushroom Gravy recipe instead of packaged gravy mix. Another alternative is to make your own beef broth or mushroom gravy. See links in the Appendix for more information.

Reviewer notes

One reviewer thought the meal was very well seasoned. She seasons her potatoes before dehydrating, so that adds some flavor as well. She bought white yams instead of sweet potatoes, but they tasted good. She included dehydrated beef from a can, as well as peas and carrots. She used about a cup of water to rehydrate and added a little more to create a more stew-like consistency. She said, "I made three portions for my group and it was delicious; I could have eaten more. That's not because the portion was too small, I just liked it and I'm always hungry when I hike."

Another reviewer said the seasoning was perfect just as listed in the recipe, stating "the sweet potato really makes this one, and it is a favorite!"

A third reviewer used only ⅛ teaspoon salt and substituted turkey gravy mix, which tasted great. She used 1.5 cups of water for the food, plus some water to reconstitute the gravy. She said, "This recipe was way better than anticipated...and my 2 daughters loved it as well."

A fourth reviewer gave the recipe a top score, but said she would not make it again as it was too complicated to assemble in the field with the ingredients packaged separately.

BBQ Chicken with Mashed Potatoes

Like the Beef Stew recipe, this is a meal I always look forward to. The BBQ sauce has such zing that it stands above many of the neutral flavors in the typical backpacking diet without being overwhelming. It's delicious.

Some brands of instant mashed potatoes are loaded with additives, especially the flavored varieties. Look for brands that contain only potatoes. Bob's Red Mill contains just one ingredient: dehydrated potatoes.

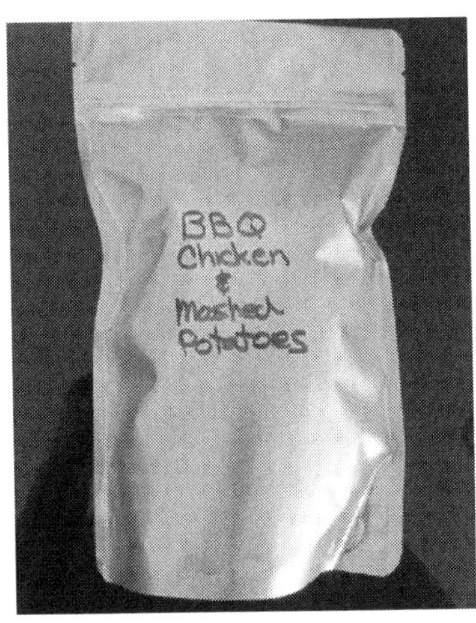

BBQ Chicken with Mashed Potatoes stored in a Mylar bag

Ingredients

¼ cup of liquid BBQ sauce dehydrated to leather (about 2 tablespoon dried)
½ cup instant mashed potato flakes
½ cup freeze-dried chicken
¼ cup freeze-dried corn
2 tablespoon freeze-dried cheddar cheese
½ tablespoon full fat powdered milk
1 tablespoon powdered butter
⅛ teaspoon salt

Black pepper to taste

Trail Staple

1 tablespoon olive oil

At home

Combine all the dry ingredients into a bag. If you want to create a layered meal, package the mashed potatoes in one bag, BBQ sauce leather in a pill pouch or small zip-top bag, and the rest of the dry ingredients in yet another bag.

In camp

Add enough hot water to cover. Start with ½-1 cup.
Add olive oil.
Stir well to moisten throughout.
Rehydrate for 10-20 minutes until softened.
Add more hot water to taste if desired.

If packaged separately, add ½ cup hot water and olive oil to the bag with the meat.
Add a small amount of hot water to the bag with BBQ sauce and gently knead it to reconstitute the sauce.
Just before serving, empty the mashed potatoes into a bowl, add ½ cup hot water and stir. Add chicken and veggies to the bowl. Top with BBQ sauce.

Yield: 1 serving
Calories 606; Carbohydrate 47 g; Protein 33 g; Fat 30 g; Sodium 959 mg

Variations

- This could be a vegetarian dish if textured vegetable protein were substituted for the chicken.
- Freeze-dried or dehydrated beef or sausage may be substituted for chicken.

- For short trips the BBQ sauce doesn't need to be dehydrated; pour the sauce into a small plastic leak-proof container.
- Quinoa flakes can be added to the mashed potatoes.
- Sweet potato bark may be substituted for mashed potatoes. See "Beef Stew with Sweet Potato Bark."
- A flavorful addition is creamed-corn bark, made by dehydrating a can of creamed corn. There is no dairy in this product; the "cream" results from the starches in the corn.

Reviewer notes

One reviewer used homemade BBQ sauce bark and guessed she probably used about ¼ cup of sauce before dehydrating. She used mashed potato bark instead of instant. She didn't taste a strong cheese flavor and suggested more cheese if desired. She used about a cup of water to rehydrate on the trail. "Flavor was very good. I will use this recipe again as it was very tasty. Optional ingredients include dried chives, shelf-stable bacon, and ranch dressing (powdered seasoning)."

Another reviewer added an extra ¼ teaspoon of salt in camp. She also made her own mashed potatoes, boiling a large potato (½ cup equivalent), before mashing and dehydrating it. She had a hard time getting the jarred BBQ sauce to dehydrate and it never turned into leather. She added the dried potatoes to the bag of chicken and rehydrated them all together. She added just enough water to cover plus a little more. She found the meal to be quite large and removed ¼ cup on the trail. "I really liked this meal and will absolutely take it with me next time I'm out. I especially liked having something that I knew would be easy on the stomach for the first night as I never feel good the first day. The BBQ sauce made for a nice aroma without overwhelming me. This was a great treat."

A third reviewer loved this recipe and so did the four kids who helped test it. She said, "This was one of our favorites. We would definitely eat this every trip and the boys would be happy, happy, happy," They wanted more BBQ sauce, though. The portions were generally good, but the boys and men in the group could have eaten another 25%.

Hearty Grits with Sausage and Veggies

This is a comfort food meal with the creamy grits and savory sausage. Reviewers were neutral on this recipe, but I kept it because in my tests my husband and a friend really liked it. I tweaked the recipe based on feedback, which has improved the flavor.

Ingredients

⅓ cup (1 ounce or 1 packet) instant (not quick-cooking) grits
¼ cup dehydrated or freeze-dried ground sausage or beef
¼ cup freeze-dried peas
3 dried shiitake mushrooms, sliced thinly
2 tablespoons freeze-dried cheddar cheese
1 tablespoon full fat powdered milk
1 teaspoon butter powder
Salt to taste (optional-may not need salt if the packaged grits contain salt)
Black pepper to taste

Trail Staple

1 tablespoon olive oil

At home

Combine all the dry ingredients into a bag.

In camp

Add enough hot water to cover the bag with meat and vegetables. Start with ½ cup.
Add olive oil.
Stir well to moisten throughout.
Rehydrate for 10-20 minutes until softened.

Just before serving, place contents of grits bag in a bowl, add ½ cup of hot water and stir.
Add meat and vegetable mixture and stir.
Add more hot water to taste if desired.

Yield: 1 serving
Calories 596; Carbohydrate 44 g; Protein 26 g; Fat 37 g; Sodium 924 mg (with no added salt)

Variations

- This can be a vegetarian dish if the meat is omitted, but it might be a bit bland. Textured vegetable protein (TVP) or other sources of protein can be added.
- Add ⅛ cup instant quinoa flakes to add some protein.
- Try different meats and vegetables. If you use a bland meat you may need to add spices (such as onion, garlic and other spices) as the sausage has its own flavor profile.
- Grated aged cheddar cheese (fresh, not freeze-dried) would give the recipe more zest if you want to carry the weight.

Reviewer notes

One reviewer "really liked this one" and thought the veggies added a lot.

Another reviewer thought the recipe was too bland and not cheesy enough, even with double the amount of cheese. She thought real cheese would improve the recipe. She added quite a bit of salt when eating it.

One reviewer had trouble getting the grits to rehydrate, though they were supposedly instant, and would try another brand. She used nearly a cup of water but since the grits didn't rehydrate it was soupy. She said, "I loved the flavor of this recipe, which really surprised me."

Mexican Black Bean and Quinoa Wrap

This is one of our staple lunches, but it works just as well for dinner. I have yet to burn out on tortillas. They go down so easily and that first bite of the soft tortilla is always delicious. Be careful of the amount of salt you put in the spice blend if you are using canned beans, commercial bean flakes or a product that contains salt instead of homemade beans with no salt added.

Tortillas will last several weeks if they are handled properly. Avoid touching them with bare hands; slide them from their original packaging into a zip-top bag if you need to repackage them. This is one time when the regular supermarket variety is preferable to preservative-free brands, which will mold quickly.

Black beans were cooked, mashed with a mallet and dehydrated

Ingredients

1 flour tortilla
½ cup dehydrated black bean or other bean flakes
¼ cup dehydrated quinoa
¼ cup freeze-dried corn
1 teaspoon Mexican Spice Blend (Chapter 10)
Salt to taste (optional)
Black pepper to taste

Optional toppings

1 teaspoon dehydrated salsa (fresh salsa dehydrated to leather)
Freeze-dried or fresh cheese
Freeze-dried ground beef or chicken (rehydrated)
Salami
Beef jerky
Tanka Bites®
Pumpkin seeds
Sunflower seeds
Roasted flax seeds
Chia seeds

Trail Staple

1 tablespoon olive oil

At home

Combine all the dry ingredients into a bag.
Store tortillas separately.

In camp

Add enough hot water to cover. Start with ½ cup. Cold water will work but may take longer.
Add olive oil.
Stir well to moisten throughout.
Rehydrate for 10-20 minutes until softened.
Add more hot water to taste if desired.

Add hot water (cold water will work but may take longer) with beans, quinoa, salsa and spices to cover. Insert in cozy for 10-20 minutes (not necessary if rehydrating at breakfast to consume at lunch). Add more water if necessary. Spread onto tortilla, top with optional toppings, roll it up and enjoy.

Yield: 1 serving for a big appetite at dinner (could be 2 servings for lunch; divide nutrition values in half)
Calories 661; Carbohydrate 94 g; Protein 23 g; Fat 21 g; Sodium 632 mg (base recipe)
Variant: Calories 834; Carbohydrate 99 g; Protein 31 g; Fat 75 g; Sodium 783 mg (base recipe plus 2 Tbsp freeze-dried cheese, 1 Tbsp sunflower seeds , 1 tsp flax seeds, 1 tsp chia seeds)

Variations

- This can be a vegetarian dish if no meat is used.
- Quinoa flakes may be substituted for dehydrated quinoa. This will provide a creamier texture and slightly different flavor. Dehydrated quinoa provides a slight crunch.
- Rice may be substituted for quinoa.
- Some natural food stores sell black bean mix in bulk bins.
- Packets of Sriracha or other hot sauce will add some zing.

Reviewer notes

One reviewer said the spice blend was just right for her taste. She likes food to be salty when hiking. She used regular flour tortillas and it made enough for two men. She used ¾ cup of water. She said, "My son and husband devoured it and really liked it. It was filling with no meat in it. It was a good hot lunch."

Another reviewer agreed that the spices were just right, though she omitted the red pepper flakes. She dehydrated ½ cup of organic black refried beans and added the corn. She split it into two meals: ⅔ for dinner and ⅓ for lunch, which worked well. She added just enough water to cover. She said, "I thought this was a great dinner and a fabulous lunch. For lunch, I just added the water to the baggie at breakfast. It was great for lunch. I also happened to have a few crushed Fritos and added them. So yummy and satisfying."

A third reviewer thought it was too salty, having used a brand of beans that was already salted. She also thought the cumin overpowered the salsa flavor. She tried it again with the salted beans and salsa with no spice blend and liked it better. She added some dehydrated quinoa. She used ¾ cup of hot water after finding that ½ cup didn't fully rehydrate the meal. She gave it a top score.

A fourth reviewer said the spices were just right. She added 1 tablespoon of freeze-dried cheddar cheese, 1 tablespoon of freeze-dried chilis, 2 tablespoons of freeze-dried corn and ¼ cup freeze-dried chicken. This made two lunch servings for her. She gave it a top score.

Chapter 12: One Pot Meal Ideas to Dehydrate

It is beyond the scope of this book to provide recipes for entire meals that can be dehydrated, but I've listed a few ideas of one-pot meals from around the world that work well. Just make a double recipe, eat half fresh and dehydrate half, or dry the whole batch.

You can find many recipes that rehydrate well online or in a cookbook. Almost any non-cheesy one-pot meal can be modified for dehydrating. The same goes for any recipe that involves a grain or pasta with a non-dairy sauce. Thick soups can work well too. Cook watery sauces or soup on the stovetop until enough liquid has boiled off to thicken, then spread on solid dehydrator tray liners or line the tray with wax paper.

Be aware that if the meal contains fat it can affect the shelf-life of dehydrated food. It's fine for short-term use (within a few weeks) but could go rancid over the long term. Use a minimal amount of oil. Cheesy meals or anything with dairy products, which contain fat, should not be dehydrated. These are best left to the professionals.

It's generally best to use foods that are in small pieces for dehydrating. Here are some examples:

- Use ground beef instead of beef cubes.
- Canned chicken dehydrates better than fresh chicken.
- Shrimp should be cut into small bits, but even better are the dried ones you can get at Asian markets (or online).
- Vegetables should be cut very small to aid the drying process.
- Small pasta such as orzo packs more efficiently than angel hair.

- Beans can be lightly mashed before dehydrating.

Lamb Stew (Photo by FiveRings)

Recipe Ideas From Around the World to Make at Home and Dehydrate

1. Texas chili (beef), Southwest (meat and bean), or vegetarian
2. Chili mac (chili with pasta)
3. Teriyaki chicken with rice or noodles
4. Asian stir fry with rice or noodles
5. Thai red curry with rice or noodles
6. Hawaiian shrimp with rice
7. Louisiana red beans with rice
8. Indian yellow curry with rice
9. Spanish paella (seafood, chicken with rice)
10. Mexican chicken mole (shredded chicken in a rich red sauce) with rice
11. Hungarian goulash (beef and vegetable stew) with mashed potatoes or pasta

12. Chicken ragu (shredded chicken in sauce with rice, mashed potatoes or orzo)
13. French cassoulet (multi-layer casserole)
14. Spaghetti (Bolognese or marinara sauce) with pasta
15. Pesto pasta
16. Shepherd's pie (cook and dehydrate meat filling) with mashed potatoes
17. Chicken with tomatoes, capers and basil with mashed potatoes
18. Inside-out Mexican enchiladas (cook and dehydrate the filling) with tortilla
19. Hearty beef stew with mashed potatoes
20. Native American Three Sisters stew (squash, beans, corn)
21. Lentil stew or soup
22. Manhattan clam chowder (with tomato base)
23. Split pea soup

Summary

- You can find recipes for whole meals to dehydrate in your collection of personal recipes, a favorite recipe book or online.
- Many one-pot meals can be dehydrated with just a few adaptations.
- Keep individual ingredients small (shredded meat, diced vegetables).
- Avoid meals with a high fat content unless they will be consumed within a short period of time.

Chapter 13: A Simple Special Occasion Dessert

Every year I see posts from people on internet hiking groups looking for special occasion ideas, perhaps a birthday or anniversary that will be celebrated on the trail. I'm not much of a dessert person and usually don't have the time to devote to preparing sweets, but it's nice to have a treat for a festive occasion.

Angel Food Cake with Strawberry Topping

Tracy Johnson submitted this simple recipe and gave me permission to use it. She recommends using very thin slices of angel food cake. Use cold water to rehydrate the fruit to retain color and texture. There are many delicious variations to this recipe.

If you have difficulty slicing the angel food cake in thin slices without it falling apart, slice thick slices, dehydrate for an hour and then cut each slice in half. When the outside gets firmer with dehydration it's easier to slice.

Ingredients

4 thin slices angel food cake, dehydrated (½ inch before dehydrating)
⅓ cup (½ of 3.4 ounce box) instant cheesecake pudding mix
⅓ cup full fat powdered milk
¼ cup (¼ ounce) dehydrated strawberries
Chocolate bar-enough to grate (optional)

At home

Combine instant pudding mix and powdered milk into a small bag.
Place angel food cake, small bag of powdered pudding/milk mix, strawberries and chocolate into a larger bag.

In camp

Add cold water to cover dried strawberries.
Add ¾ - 1 cup cold water (depending on consistency desired) to pudding mixture and stir vigorously for 2 minutes.
Pour a dollop of cheesecake on a plate. If the mixture is too thick, add more water.
Place the angel food cake on top. Pour the rest of the cheesecake mixture over angel food cake. Let it sit for a few minutes to rehydrate the cake.
Top with rehydrated strawberries.
Grate chocolate over the top with a knife edge.

Yield: 2 servings
Calories per serving 294; Carbohydrate 52 g; Protein 7 g; Fat 6 g; Sodium 636 mg

Variations

- Substitute other berries, such as blueberry or raspberry, for the topping.
- Use dehydrated pound cake instead of angel food cake. Due to the oils in pound cake it is suitable for short term storage.
- Instead of slices, cake "croutons" can be made by cutting the cake into small pieces.
- For a tropical twist, use banana cream or coconut pudding mix and tropical fruits, such as chopped, dried mango or pineapple or rehydrated banana chips.

- Other pudding mixes can be substituted for cheesecake pudding, including vanilla, chocolate, fudge, flan, caramel or pumpkin.
- Chocolate or strawberry milk powder can be mixed with water to create a drizzle instead of using the grated chocolate.
- Honey, stored in a straw with each end sealed, can be drizzled over the top of flan or vanilla pudding. These honey-filled tubes can also be purchased.
- Instead of using angel food cake as the base, bring graham crackers and sugar in a bag. On the trail, mix with a bit of olive oil or ghee to make a crust for the bottom instead of the cake, or crumble on top of the pudding.

Angel Food Cake (Photo by Tracy Johnson)

Chapter 14: Resupply Strategy

Your resupply strategy will depend on the length of the trail you are hiking and the nuances of that trail. For example, many stops along the Appalachian Trail are in towns that have restaurants and grocery stores so mailed supplies are less important than on the Pacific Crest Trail. On the PCT, towns are sometimes located many miles from the trail across rugged terrain. See the Pacific Crest Trail Association and Appalachian Trail Conservancy for more information on resupply strategies. Resupply locations on the Continental Divide Trail are available on Soruck.net.

Resupply stops offer an important opportunity to add some variety, taste, texture and nutrition during the time you're there, whether it's a brief stop or a full rest day. For mailed resupplies, think about adding some food treats as well as toiletries and other luxuries. Also think about changing things up a bit for the next stretch, in case you're getting bored with some of your food choices. Start introducing new flavors and toppings.

Also, take into consideration how your body will be responding to days and days on the trail. Many people find that they aren't that hungry the first week. You can usually go lighter that week, but make sure you're upping the calories for the second week and beyond.

An alternative to preparing and mailing your own supplies is to use one of the services that assemble your desired items from a list and mail them to the locations you designate. These include Sonora Pass Resupply (located in Northern California) and Zero Day Resupply (located in New Hampshire). Some hikers use online delivery services such as Amazon Pantry to deliver supplies.

Resupply stops may provide an opportunity to pick up some delectable fresh foods such as this deli assortment in France

Resupply Foods to Pack

If you're taking a full zero day, you are likely to have five meals at your resupply location: dinner upon arrival, breakfast, lunch and dinner on your zero day, and breakfast the morning you depart. Early in your trip you may be at a location where you can get hot meals, such as Tuolumne Meadows or Red's Meadow on the JMT/PCT, though not all the places have a restaurant or store. Take advantage of that and plan to eat your meals there. After Red's Meadow the only place you can get a meal is Vermillion Valley Resort unless you are paying for a cabin at Muir Trail Ranch. If there isn't going be a place to purchase food you can include some treats for yourself. You can pack heavy items like tuna pouches, canned foods, chips, cookies—anything shelf stable. The only constraint is space. We sent two five-gallon buckets to MTR for two people. The contents of most of one bucket was just for our zero day meals while the other contained our food for the next ten days. Even so, I couldn't pack all of the goodies that I had wanted because they wouldn't fit.

For one resupply dinner, we rehydrated one of my home-dehydrated meals that was delicious but incredibly bulky. The angel hair pasta just wouldn't smash down so we ate the Asian Chicken Salad during our rest day. For another dinner, we opened two cans of Amy's Organic Chili, which is vegetarian, and added chunks of chicken from foil pouches. We didn't have a pot, so we heated water in the JetBoil put the chili in a bag and placed the bag in a hot water bath. It was warm enough and tasted mighty fine.

Casey Cox, who owns Sonora Pass Resupply, provided this list of the top ten items that long-distance hikers order for resupply:

1. Snickers bars
2. Clif or other bars
3. Freeze-dried meals
4. Instant mashed potatoes or side dishes
5. Ramen
6. Tortillas
7. Oatmeal
8. Tuna or salmon packets
9. Cheese
10. Instant refried beans

A huge benefit of resupply stops is the overflow area. Usually a bucket, box or line of buckets contains foods and other items that backpackers are abandoning. If you're backpacking at peak season you may find a plethora of items that you can use. We exchanged a few things we were sick of in favor of some tuna packets we found. In particular, the hiker barrels at MTR are legendary: more than 20 labeled buckets contain homemade foods, commercial dinners, lunches, snacks, sundries, maps, batteries, socks and more as backpackers dump weight and realize they can't pack everything they sent into their backpack.

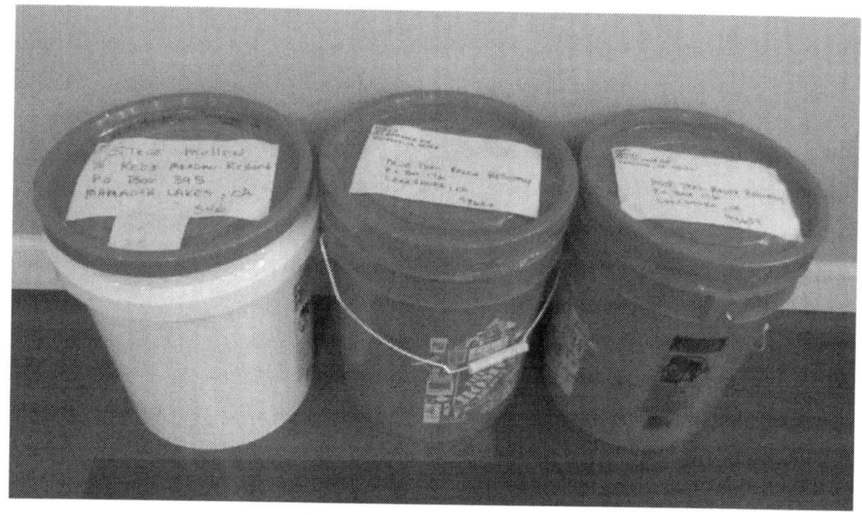

Resupply buckets are ready for shipping

Resupply Treat Ideas

- UHT milk-boxes (regular, chocolate, strawberry)
- Cheese
- Cookies
- Tortilla chips
- Potato chips
- Smoked trout
- Sardines
- Kippers
- Canned peaches
- Canned corn
- Canned peas
- Dried fruit
- Tuna packets
- Chicken pouches or canned chicken
- Canned chili or stew
- Breakfast meals (freeze-dried) or powdered eggs
- Shelf-stable bacon
- Salami

Non-food items:

- Socks
- Razor
- Shampoo/conditioner
- Lotion
- Extra zip-top bags

Resupply Requirements

Each place that handles a resupply may have their own specifications for the type of packaging they will accept, the amount of time they will hold a package, what kind of information is on the mailing label and how far in advance they recommend mailing. They may require that you use their label. Some remote ranches are only operational during the summer season and have different opening and closing dates. Some proprietors charge a fee for pickup and storage. These fees are in addition to any shipping fees from the U.S. Postal Service (USPS) or private shippers such as UPS or FedEx. Some locations are only serviced by the USPS or private shipper, but not both. Be sure you understand the requirements and plan for them.

To illustrate the differences, the specific requirements for several resupply ranches along the PCT are included below (these requirements can change so check the websites for current information).

Muir Trail Ranch (MTR), located at the half-way point on the JMT

- They only accept five-gallon or smaller plastic buckets (not cardboard boxes).
- They are generally open mid-June to mid-September (check website for dates).

- You pay a resupply fee online (this is separate from the postage fee you will pay at the post office) and then a mailing label is generated. You can print the label and tape it to the bucket.
- You will receive a claim ticket. Keep the claim ticket with you or store an image of it on a device so you can show it to the staff at MTR.
- They recommend USPS Priority Mail. UPS and Fed Ex will not deliver to their P.O. Box.
- Mail 3 weeks before your pickup date.

Resupply at MTR on table; note hiker barrels in background full of discarded food and supplies

Vermillion Valley Ranch (VVR), located about 20 miles north of MTR near the JMT.

- They accept boxes or plastic buckets.
- They are generally open mid-May to mid-October (check website for dates).

- You pay a resupply fee (this is separate from the postage fee you will pay).
- They prefer UPS but will accept USPS.
- Mail so that the package arrives within 10-14 days of your pickup date.

Red's Meadow Resort and Pack Station, located near the town of Mammoth Lakes, CA.

- They accept boxes or plastic buckets.
- They are generally open mid-June to September 30 or earlier (check website for dates).
- You pay a resupply fee (this is separate from the postage fee you will pay). Complete a form (available on their website), pay by credit card and mail separately to Red's Meadow Resort.
- Use USPS only. UPS and Fed Ex will not deliver to their P.O. Box.
- Mail so that the package arrives several days prior to your pickup date.

Resupply bucket at Red's Meadow Resort

Kennedy Meadows Resort, located 10 miles from the PCT near Sonora, CA.

- Use UPS only.
- Resupply boxes are held in the store.
- Include your name and estimated date of arrival on the box.
- A fee is charged per box.

Resupply to post offices, persons or businesses

Resupply containers may also be sent to hiker-friendly motels (if you plan to stay there), stores or trail angel locations. Trail angels are people who choose to perform acts of kindness for hikers (see trail angel lists at Trailangellist.org). These businesses may or may not charge a fee. Post-offices accept resupplies, too, in the form of "general delivery." Packages will generally be held for 30 days.

See below for the format to use for USPS General Delivery. Write "Please hold for hiker" and your "ETA" or estimated date of arrival. Complete the label in a similar way for other mailing, but substitute "C/O (name of person or business accepting your package)" for "General Delivery."

Name (your name)
General Delivery
City Name, State
Zip Code

"Please hold for hiker"
"ETA: XX/XX/XXXX (date expected)"

If you have multiple resupply points it's a good idea to print each set of requirements and have them available as you assemble your food cache.

For multi-month thru-hikes you will likely be depending on others to mail your cache.

Summary

- Package your resupply foods and other items in a box or plastic bucket; check with the entity accepting the resupply package for specific requirements.
- Add some favorite food treats in your resupply for immediate consumption.
- Read, understand and print the mailing instructions for each resupply entity.
- Resupply packages may be sent to post offices as general delivery.
- Some businesses will accept resupply deliveries.

Steve enjoys a big Hiker Breakfast at the Whitney Portal Store after completing the High Sierra Trail. No matter how good your trail food is, nothing can substitute for a real meal at the end of a hike.

Appendix 1: Resources

Recipes

Braaten, Brenda PhD, RD. "**Pack Light, Eat Right**." *Thru-Hiker: Gear and Resources for Long Distance Hikers.* Thru-Hiker.com. Web, accessed 1/8/2017.
(See "Recipes" link)

Conners, Tim and Conners, Christine. ***Lipsmackin' Backpackin': Lightweight, Trail-Tested Recipes for Backcountry Trips.*** Helena, MT: Three Forks Press, 2000. Print.
(Contains recipes from real thru-hikers of America's long trails)

McAllister, Glenn. ***Backpacking Food for the Soul.*** BackpackingChef.com. Web, accessed 1/8/2017.
(Glenn McAllister, who wrote the book, "Recipes for Adventure" listed below, has a comprehensive website with dehydrating instructions and recipes)

McAllister, Glenn. ***Recipes for Adventure: Healthy, Hearty & Homemade Backpacking Recipes.*** Waleska, GA: Glenn McAllister, 2013. Print.
(Contains detailed instructions with full color photos on how to dehydrate food)

Monica Matheny. "**Six Instant Meals on the Go**." *The Yummy Life-Easy, Healthy, Delicious Recipes.* TheYummyLife.com. Web, accessed 1/8/2017.
(A hiker's wife presents a week's worth of freezer-bag recipes that are tasty and nutritious)

Nutrition

Asorson, Erik. "**Five Day Lightweight Backpacking Meal Plan**." *Erik the Black's Backpacking Blog.* BlackwoodsPress.com. Web, accessed 1/8/2017. (*Erik provides spreadsheets for 5 days of food with approximately 3,500 calories in 2 pounds per day, broken out by ounces, calories and calories per ounce)*

Bennett, Brad L. et al. "**Wilderness Medical Society Practice Guidelines for Treatment of Exercise-Associated Hyponatremia: 2014 Update**." *Wilderness & Environmental Medicine*, www.wemjournal.org. Dec. 2014, Volume 25, Issue 4, S30 - S42. Web, accessed 1/8/2017.
(The experts from the Wilderness Medical Society provide information about the dangers of over-hydration, which can lead to dangerously low levels of blood sodium)

BMI Calculator. BMICalculator.net. Web, accessed 1/8/2017.
(Find Basal Metabolic Rate (BMR) and Harris-Benedict Calculators to determine calorie needs based on height, weight and activity level)

Braaten, Brenda PhD, RD. "**Pack Light, Eat Right**." *Thru-Hiker: Gear and Resources for Long Distance Hikers.* Thru-Hiker.com. Web. accessed 1/8/2017.
(See individual sections for formulas to calculate carbohydrate, fat and protein needs)

Deuster, Patricia A; Kemmer, Teresa; Tubbs, Lori, et. al. United States, Department of Defense. ***The Special Operations Forces Nutrition Guide-Warrior Athlete, Fueling the Human Weapon, Nutrient Timing, Healthy Snacking, Keeping Lean, Bulking Up, Combat Rations, Nutrition for Combat.*** Government Printing Office. Web (PDF), accessed 1/8/2017. (Kindle Edition available)
(This document is packed with information about nutrition, caloric needs,

nutrient timing, hydration and more; enter the title in your browser to locate a PDF)

Eng, Ronald C., ed. "**Camping and Food**." Mountaineering: Freedom of the Hills, 8th Ed. Seattle, WA: The Mountaineers Books. 2010. Print.
(Good overview of food and water requirements in an alpine environment)

"**Fiber Content of Foods in Common Portions.**" *Harvard University Health Services.* Web (PDF), accessed 1/21/2017.
(List of food and fiber content; *enter the title in your browser to locate a PDF)*

"Freeze-dried Food vs Dehydrated." *The Ready Store.* Thereadystore.com. Web, accessed 1/21/2017.
(Describes the process and nutritional value of freeze-dried and dehydrated commercial foods)

Hauser, Michelle, MD. MPA. "**Make Your Own Gatorade, Stay Hydrated, Get Running**." *Chef In Residency.* Chefinresidency.com. Apr. 16, 2012. Web, accessed 1/21/2017.
(A chef, doctor and runner shares tips, including this recipe for a DIY electrolyte solution)

Lichter, Justin (aka "Trauma"). "**Trail Food**." *Tail Tested: A Thru-Hiker's Guide to Ultralight Hiking and Backpacking. Helena,* MT: FalconGuides. 2013. Print.
(Good overview of food requirements for long-distance backpacking)

Ryan, Mary Howley, MS, RD. ***NOLS Backcountry Nutrition, Eating Beyond the Basics.*** Mechanicsburg, PA: Stackpole Books. July 21, 2008. Print. 2008.

Skolnik, Heide and Chernus, Andrea. ***Nutrient Timing for Peak Performance.*** Champaign, IL: Human Kinetics. 2010. Print.

(In depth information about how nutrients are metabolized and how to tailor food to physiologic needs)

Skurka, Andrew. "**Food**." *The Ultimate Hiker's Gear Guide: Tools and Techniques to Hit the Trail, 2nd Ed.* Washington, DC: National Geographic. Print.
(Good overview of food requirements for long-distance backpacking)

United States, Departments of the Army, Navy and Air Force. ***Nutrition and Standards Education. US Army Bulletin. Army Regulation 40-25.*** **Government Printing Office**. June 15, 2001. BUMEDINST 101110.6. AFI 44-141.
(See Table 2.1 for calorie needs at varying levels per US Army. If the link doesn't work, enter the title in your browser to locate a PDF)

Dehydration Food Safety

"Dehydrating Ground Beef Safely." *Real Food Living.* Realfoodliving.com. Web, accessed 1/21/17.
(Contains instructions for dehydrating meats, however, refer to government and university sites below for storage and shelf life information)

"**Dehydrator Info-Graphic Charts**." *21st Century Simple Living.* 21stcenturysimpleliving.com. Web, accessed 1/21/17.
(Includes pre-treatment and drying temperature info)

"Food Preservation and Storage," *Purdue Extension, Purdue University.* Mdc.itap.purdue.edu. Web, accessed 1/21/17.
(Several articles on safe dehydration practices.

"**Food Safety: Drying**." *University of Minnesota Extension.* Extension.umn.edu/food/food-safety/preserving/drying/. Web, accessed 1/21/17.
(This is a good site for learning the basics about food safety)

"**How Do I Dry**?" *National Center for Home Food Preservation.* Nchfp.uga.edu/how/dry. Web, accessed 1/21/17.
(*This site has lots of information about drying specific food items such as fruits, vegetables and meats*)

Drying your own produce can be fun and cost-effective

"**Jerky and Food Safety.**" *USDA.* Fsis.usda.gov. Web, accessed 1/21/17.
(Commercially packaged jerky can be kept 12 months; home-dried jerky can be stored 1 to 2 months)

"**Making Safe Jerky in a Home Dehydrator**." *University of Wisconsin.* Foodsafety.wisc.edu. Web, accessed 1/21/17. (PDF document available)

(Learn how to dehydrate meat properly to kill pathogens such as salmonella and E.coli)

"**Storage Considerations for Dried Foods**." *21st Century Simple Living.* 21stcenturysimpleliving.com. Web, accessed 1/21/17.
(Useful info about storage containers, oxygen absorbers and desiccant packets)

General Food Safety

"**Bacon and Food Safety**." *United States Department of Agriculture, Food Safety and Inspection Service.* Fsis.usda.gov. Web, accessed 3/21/27.
(See chart with safe time limits for various forms of bacon)

"Does All Cheese Need to be Refrigerated?" *United States Department of Agriculture, Food Safety and Inspection Service.* Fsis.usda.gov. Web, accessed 3/21/27.
(Hard cheeses such as cheddar, processed cheeses (American), and both block and grated Parmesan do not require refrigeration)

"Freeze-dried Food vs Dehydrated." *The Ready Store.* Thereadystore.com. Web, accessed 1/21/2017.
(Describes the process and nutritional value of freeze-dried and dehydrated commercial foods)

"How Long Does Dehydrated or Freeze-Dried Food Last After Opening?" *Be Prepared Blog.* Beprepared.com/blog/.Web, accessed 3/21/2017.

(Discussion on variables affecting shelf life. This is a corporate blog, not a government site, so use the information at your discretion.)

"Molds On Food: Are They Dangerous?" *United States Department of Agriculture, Food Safety and Inspection Service.* Fsis.usda.gov. Web, accessed 3/21/27.

"**Sausages and Food Safety**." *United States Department of Agriculture, Food Safety and Inspection Service.* Fsis.usda.gov. Web, accessed 3/21/27. (Hard/dry sausages, such as Genoa salami, sopressata and pepperoni, are shelf-stable for 6 weeks if whole.)

"**The Everlasting Tortilla**." *Packit Gourmet Blog.* Packitgourmet.com. Web, accessed 1/21/17.
(See the results of a 35-day test with three tortilla brands)

"Vacuum Seal." *BackpackingChef.com.* Backpackingchef.com. Web, accessed 1/21/17.
(Information on vacuum sealing food

Appendix 2: Food Sources Listed by Purveyor

Note: All food sources have websites.

Amazon (many of the products listed below are available on Amazon)

Bob's Red Mill (instant potato flakes, gluten-free products, grains, etc)

Clif Bar (large variety of organic bars with gluten-free, soy-free, kosher and low-glycemic choices)

Mountain House (freeze dried backpacking meals and bulk #10 cans)

Backpacker's Pantry (freeze dried backpacking meals and bulk #10 cans)

Fantastic foods (buy dry food and mixes direct from the source commonly used to stock bulk bins at natural food stores)

Gu Energy Labs (hydration mix and other energy products)

Harmony House (tomato powder, freeze dried ingredients, dry soup blends, textured vegetable protein, no additives or preservatives, vegan choices)

Hawk Vittles (gourmet, no artificial flavors or preservatives, lower sodium)

Honeyville (freeze dried bulk foods, including meat, veg, fruit, eggs and dairy with no or minimal additives)

Karen's Naturals (freeze-dried fruits and vegetables with no additives; previously known as Just Tomatoes)

Koyo Ramen (healthy ramen)

Krave Jerky (no MSG, nitrates, nitrates or corn syrup)

Lotus Foods (rice ramen noodles with or without soup mixes, gluten free)

Macro Bar (vegan, macrobiotic, gluten-free energy bars)

MaryJane's Farm Organics (freeze dried organic backpacking meals and bulk foods)

Minimus.biz for condiments (e.g. Sriracha sauce, mustard, mayonnaise, etc.) and a wide range of other foods in individual packets

Outdoor Herbivore (vegetarian and vegan)

OvaEasy egg crystals and egg white protein powder

Pack It Gourmet (backpacking foods including vegetarian, vegan, low sodium, diary-free, gluten-free, dairy, sauces, individual packets and meals)

Paleo Meals To Go (Paleo backpacking meals and more; freeze-dried, gluten free, grain free, milk free, soy free, protein-rich, and shelf-stable)

PROBAR (flavorful organic energy bars)

Santa Fe Bean Company (dehydrated bean mixes)

Star Anise Foods (brown rice Happy Pho noodles, gluten free; no MSG)

Skratch Labs (hydration mix–all natural products)

Stash Tea Honey Sticks (plain and flavored)

Tanka Bars Bars, Bites and Jerky (buffalo & cranberry with no MSG, nitrates, nitrates or hormones)

Taste Adventure (vegan bulk bean flakes and soup mixes)

The Spice Tin (large variety of small quantities of spices, including Umami Dust Seasoning).

Thrive Life (freeze-dried meats and cheese, instant beans, fruit, vegetables, honey crystals)

Trader Joe's Stores (freeze-dried fruit and other backpacker-friendly food, no MSG in any store-labeled product)

True Citrus (pure citrus crystals for flavoring water and recipes)

Woodland Foods (fruit and vegetable powders including mushroom powder, chili powder, Umami Dust Seasoning, edible insects, insect powder, bean powder and other foods)

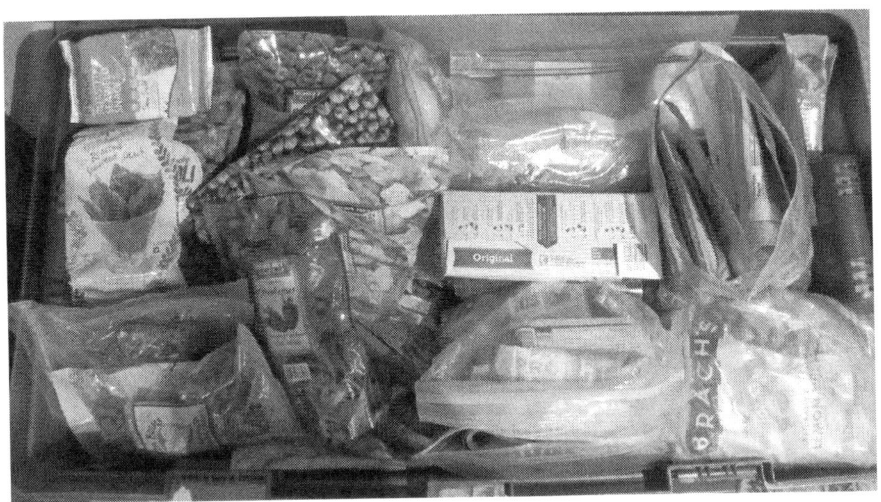

Box of backpacking food

Appendix 3: Food Sources Listed by Food

Note: All food sources have websites.

Bean flakes, dehydrated. Available at Santa Fe Bean Company, Harmony House, Amazon (various brands), natural food stores and other retailers.

Beef, freeze-dried. See *Meat.*

Butter powder. Available at Honeyville, Packit Gourmet, Amazon and other retailers.

Buttermilk powder. Available at Honeyville, Amazon and other retailers.

Cheese, freeze-dried (cheddar, parmesan and other). Available at Honeyville, Packit Gourmet, Amazon and other retailers.

Chicken, freeze-dried. Available from Honeyville, Mountain House, Packit Gourmet, Amazon and other retailers.

Citrus fruit powders (pure powders, including lemon and lime, with no additives). Available from True Citrus and Minimus.biz

Coconut Cream Powder. Chao Thai brand, one of many, is available at Amazon and other retailers.

Condiments (individual packets that can be purchased individually). Available at Minimus.biz.

Cream cheese powder. Available at Honeyville, Amazon and other retailers.

Dairy powders. Available at Honeyville, Packit Gourmet, Amazon and other retailers.

Egg powder. OvaEasy egg crystals are available at Amazon. Powdered eggs are available at Honeyville and other retailers.

Fruit, freeze-dried and dehydrated (grape, blueberry, strawberry, raspberry, mango, banana, pineapple, coconut, etc.). Available from Honeyville, Karen's Naturals, Harmony House, Amazon, Trader Joe's and other retailers.

Furikake (sesame seeds and seaweed flakes). Nori Komi (does not have MSG) and other brands available at Amazon, Asian food stores and other retailers.

Grits, instant. Quaker brand available at Amazon and supermarkets in some regions.

Honey packets or sticks. Available at Minimus.biz, Amazon and other retailers.

Hummus mix, dehydrated. Available from multiple online retailers and supermarkets including Amazon.

Jams and preserves individual packets. Available at Minimus.biz.

Ketchup packets. See *Condiments.*

Lemon, lime or other fruit powders. See *Citrus*.

Noodles-brown rice. Happy Pho noodles available from Star Anise Foods at natural food and specialty grocery stores.

Meat, freeze-dried. Available from Honeyville, Thrive Life, Mountain House, Amazon and other retailers.

Milk powder, whole milk. Nido or Peak brands are available from multiple retailers at Amazon.

Mustard packets. See *Condiments.*

Mayonnaise packets. See *Condiments.*

Mushroom powder. Available at Woodland Foods and Amazon.

Mushroom seasoning. PoLoKu brand available at Amazon (unable to verify all ingredients).

Noodles–wheat ramen (no MSG or preservatives). Available from Koyo Natural Foods, Amazon, other online retailers and specialty grocery stores.

Noodles–white or black rice ramen (no MSG or preservatives). Available from Lotus Foods (rice ramen noodles with or without soup mixes)

Peanut butter powder. PB2 brand available at Amazon and other retailers.

Potato flakes (instant mashed potatoes). Available at Bob's Red Mill (no additives or preservatives), Amazon and other retailers.

Quinoa flakes. Available at Amazon and natural food stores.

Rice (freeze-dried). Available at Outdoor Herbivore.

Sausage, freeze-dried. Available from Honeyville, Packit Gourmet, Thrive Life, Amazon and other retailers.

Seaweed (dried roasted sheets of seaweed known as *nori*). Sea's Gift and other brands available at many supermarkets, Amazon and other online retailers.

Sriracha sauce and other hot sauce packets. See *Condiments.*

Sour cream powder. Available at Honeyville.

Spices. Available at The Spice Tin in small packages, Amazon and other retailers.

Sweet potato, freeze-dried. Available at Honeyville, Harmony House, Amazon and other retailers.

Tanka Bars Bites, jerky and bars (buffalo & cranberry with no MSG, nitrates, nitrates or hormones)

Tabbouleh mix. Near East, Fantastic Foods or other brands are available at Amazon, supermarkets and other retailers.

Tomato powder. Available from Harmony House, Amazon and other retailers.

Vegetable powder. Available from Woodland Foods.

Vegetables, freeze-dried and dehydrated (green bean, broccoli, tomato, corn, pea, etc.). Available from Honeyville, Karen's Naturals, Harmony House, Amazon, Trader Joe's and other retailers.

Umami Dust Seasoning (provides a meaty robust flavor to soups and stews). Available at The Spice Tin, Amazon, Woodland Foods or other online retailers.

Appendix 4: Non-Food Products

Some products, such as stoves, are produced by many manufacturers and preferences are very personal. Others, such as bear canisters, may be regulated by wilderness agencies. This is a list of products mentioned in the book but many other brands and styles are available for most types of items. All sources have websites.

Ball Freezer Jars, plastic with caps, 8 oz. Available from Amazon and stores that stock canning supplies.

Bear bag, Ursack. Available at Ursack, Amazon and other retailers.

Bear canister, Bearikade. Available from Wild Ideas.

Bear canister, BearVault. Available at REI, Amazon and other retailers.

Bear canister, Garcia Backpacker Food Cache. Available at REI, Amazon and other retailers.

Bowls, polypropylene. Available from GSI, Amazon and other retailers.

Bowls and cups, titanium, in different sizes. Available from Toaks, Amazon and other retailers.

Collapsible bottles, Platypus SoftBottle or Hydrapak SoftFlask. Available at Amazon, REI and other retailers.

Dehydrator, Nesco. Available at Amazon and other retailers.

Dehydrator, Excalibur. Available at Amazon and other retailers.

Food cozy (insulated bag to keep food warm while rehydrating). Available at Amazon or other online retailers.

Food cozy DIY Instructions:

1. "DIY Designer Freezer Bag Stand up Cozy" instructions on YouTube.
2. "MYOG Freezer Bag Cozy" instructions for a simple cozy from SectionHiker.com.
3. "Ultralight Backpacking Pot Cozy" instructions from Erik the Black

Food Saver Vacuum Sealer machine. Available at Amazon, CostCo and other retailers.

Jars, Ball Freezer Jars, plastic with caps, 8 oz. Available from Amazon and stores that stock canning supplies.

Kitchen scale, Oxo Good Grips 5-lb scale. Available at Amazon and other retailers.

Mug, insulated, polypropylene. Infinity Backpacker Mug available at GSI Outdoors, REI, Amazon and other retailers.

Pill Pouch-3x2" (The Pill Bag, EZY Dose, or other brand, used for storing spices and dehydrated leathers, such as salsa—look for the thicker 3 mil or 4 mil plastic). Available at Amazon or retail pharmacies.

Opsak plastic bags for storing and rehydrating food. Available at Amazon, REI or other sporting goods stores.

Oxygen absorber packets. Available from Amazon and other retailers.

Mylar bags (foil bags like the kind used by commercial backpacking food companies). Available at Amazon.

Stove, JetBoil. Available at JetBoil, REI, Amazon and other retailers.

Stove, MSR Pocket Rocket or Pocket Rocket 2. Available at MSR, REI, Amazon and other retailers.

Utensil, foldable. Available from MSR, Toaks, REI, Amazon and other retailers.

Utensil, spork. Available from REI, Amazon and other retailers.

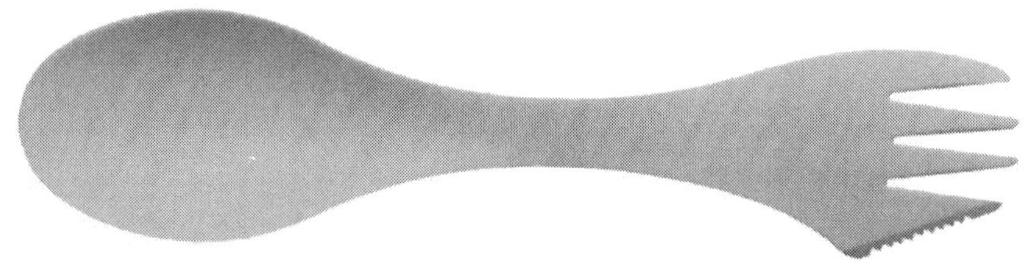

Spork

Disclaimer: I may earn a small commission for links to any products from Amazon. I am a participant in the Amazon Services LLC Associates Program, an affiliate advertising program designed to provide a means for sites to earn advertising fees by advertising and linking to Amazon. I get a few cents for products purchased through this link. It is not a big moneymaker at the moment, but who knows; I may get rich and be able to quit my day job someday.

Appendix 5: Glycemic Index (GI)

The following are examples of the glycemic index of typical backpacker foods.

Low Glycemic Index (<=55)

- Fructose
- Beans (kidney, black, red, lentil, chickpea, etc)
- Seeds
- Nuts
- Barley
- Whole oats
- Many vegetables
- Many fruits
- Mushrooms
- Whole grain bread
- Corn tortilla
- Wheat tortilla
- All Bran
- Pasta-can be low or medium GI
- Rice noodles-can be low or medium GI
- Udon noodles
- Dates
- Chocolate
- Brown rice
- Red rice
- Instant pudding

- Chips
- Peanut M&Ms
- Granola bars-can be low or medium GI
- Energy/protein bars-can be low or medium GI
- Nutella
- Peanut butter
- Fruit juice
- Milk
- Peak full-fat milk
- Soy milk
- Rice milk
- Hot chocolate with water
- Malted milk powder with milk
- Milo powder with water or milk

Medium Glycemic Index (56-69)

- Sucrose or white sugar
- Pita bread
- Basmati rice
- Raisins
- Banana
- Whole wheat bread
- Muesli
- Raisin Bran
- Brown rice
- Couscous
- Corn
- Honey
- Pasta-can be low or medium GI
- Rice noodles-can be low or medium GI
- Granola bars--can be low or medium GI

- Energy/protein bars-can be low or medium GI

High Glycemic Index (>69)

- Dextrose, glucose
- High fructose corn syrup
- White bread
- Bagel
- Pretzel
- Many breakfast cereals, such as Grape Nuts, Corn Flakes
- Instant oatmeal
- Instant Cream of Wheat
- Instant Grits
- Maltodextrins
- Sweet potato
- White potatoes
- White rice
- Watermelon
- Instant potatoes
- Rice crackers
- Jasmine rice
- Instant rice
- Tang
- Gatorade
- Jelly beans
- M&Ms

Appendix 6: Other Links

Inga's Adventures, ingasadventures.com

The Hungry Spork Data Sheets (spreadsheets with nutritional breakdown for individual recipes), bit.ly/HungrySporkDataSheets.

Facebook Groups

- Backcountry Meal Planning for Thru Hikers
- Nutrition for Hikers
- Dehydrating Divas and Dudes

About the Author

Inga Aksamit is a Northern California travel writer who has a passion for adventure and exploration. She loves nature so she gets out whenever she can to hike, backpack, ski, mountain bike and paddle, but when she's done, she likes to eat well. She's been backpacking for more than 15 years, honing her approach to meal planning and creating tasty, wholesome recipes that require minimal effort on the trail. She volunteers at local state parks, teaches backpacking classes and guides backpacking trips for the Sierra Club. She and her husband split their time between their home base in Sonoma County and Lake Tahoe.

Publications include *The Hungry Spork: A Long Distance Hiker's Guide to Meal Planning* and *Highs and Lows on the John Muir Trail*, as well as stories in anthologies and magazines including *Travel Stories from Around the Globe, Coast and Kayak Magazine, A Taste of Travel*, and *Journeys: On the Road & Off the Map.* Her website, Inga's Adventures (www.Inga's Adventures.com), is loaded with backpacking tips, trip reports, gear reviews and other resources.

Inga at Echo Lake in Desolation Wilderness (Photo by Steve Mullen)

Thank You for Reading

If you enjoyed "The Hungry Spork," please write a short review on Amazon. Your feedback is valuable to me.

To contact me or follow my adventures, see my website, Inga's Adventures (ingasadventures.com). I'd love to hear from you and am happy to answer any questions.

Follow me on Facebook at Inga's Adventures. I'm active on a number of Facebook Groups, including John Muir Trail, Ladies of the JMT, Backcountry Meal Planning for Thru Hikers, and California Backpacking Women.

Follow me on Twitter @IngaAksamit.

Made in the USA
San Bernardino, CA
12 November 2019